Poetry:
the Nottingham
Collection

Edited by John Lucas

Five Leaves Publications

www.fiveleaves.co.uk

Poetry: the Nottingham Collection

Published in 2005 by Five Leaves Publications,
PO Box 81, Nottingham NG5 4ER
info@fiveleaves.co.uk, www.fiveleaves.co.uk

ISBN 0 907123 236

Five Leaves gratefully acknowledges financial support
from Arts Council England

Cover illustration: Sky Mirror, photograph
©Martine Hamilton Knight
www.builtvision.co.uk

Printed by Russell Press, Nottingham
Typeset and design by Four Sheets Design and Print

Contents

Foreword

In 1812, the Newcastle-upon-Tyne bookseller John Bell had printed for him an anthology with the portmanteau title *Rhymes of Northern Bards: Being a Curious Collection of Old and New Songs Peculiar to the Counties of Newcastle upon Tyne, Northumberland and Durham.* Bell sank over £100 in the project and was amply repaid when the edition of 400 copies quickly sold out at six shillings a copy. You might think that this success would have encouraged a reprint, perhaps several. But no. In his long introduction to the facsimile edition of 1971, published in an edition of 950 copies by another Newcastle publisher, Frank Graham, David Harker says that Bell's anthology was lost to sight until Graham agreed to re-publication. Why? I suspect because Bell had wider interests and that these fully occupied him. Born in 1755, he was one of those 18th century men of wide-ranging intellectual curiousity who were such a feature of provincial England at that time, and quite apart from his bookselling business he took a keen interest in, among other matters, collecting and antiquarianism. As a result he busied himself with a variety of publishing ventures, many of them celebrating the history of the North East and its writers. But *Rhymes of Northern Bards* went into the dark.

Bell's anthology was not the first of its kind, nor would it be the last. What gave it an especial distinction was Bell's concern for work "peculiar" to the geographic area on which he drew. He looked especially for poems and songs that celebrated local customs, and wherever possible he made sure that the printed versions honoured regional dialect (and therefore phonetic spelling). This set the pattern for later anthologies, from those in the 19th century that brought together writings of the industrial north-west or which drew on the rural south, to more recent, 20th century compilations. *The Nottingham Collection* doesn't, however, follow this pattern. It aims instead to print poems by writers who have been at some time associated with the city and its environs, no more, no less. If this seems unduly permissive it is also the point, for it recognises that ideas of "rootedness" and "the local" on which these earlier anthologies depended, and which their compilers may indeed have hoped to take for granted, can scarcely apply to a modern city where heterogeneity is as inevitable as it is to be desired. In this all-important sense, *The Nottingham Collection* is, we hope, an apt anthology for the early 21st century.

It is also contemporary and, largely, by living poets. In our early planning we discussed whether to include samples from the local poetry heritage, Byron and D.H. Lawrence standing at the front of a very long queue to get in. But we decided to leave that task to others. Similarly, we decided to include only those who write in English, feeling unqualified to select from the network of local poets writing solely in Urdu, Punjabi and other minority languages.

There are three significant presses associated with Nottingham: Shoestring, Five Leaves and a relative newcomer, Leafe Press, and the Acknowledgments indicate that many of our poets have found a home in one or other of these presses. This collection, which marks the tenth anniversary of Five Leaves Publications, is published in company with *Sunday Night and Monday Morning* — a collection of fiction by fifteen contemporary writers. Anyone familiar with Nottingham will understand the title. Unlike many small presses, however, Five Leaves' concerns are wide, Jewish secular culture, social history, Catalonia, allotments... and to take us back to where this introduction started, Five Leaves will, next year, take over the long-standing Iron Press, publishing writers from the North East. My own press, Shoestring, and Five Leaves operate in friendly rivalry — long may this continue.

John Lucas

C.J. Allen

Love on a Farm Boy's Wages

I have fought my way through the hedge
for you. I have stolen flowers.
I am probably standing too close.

I have come to ask you out.
So will you come out with me?
We could walk along the hedgerows.

We could try and keep in step.
We could just see what it feels like.
We could talk about whatever you wanted.

We could catch the bus to the next village.
We could agree there is virtually nothing
to do in a dump like this.

After all, you and I are alike.
We are similarly alienated.
We are both unsure quite what that means.

We would both like Sky Digital.
So will you come out with me?
I've ruined my good shoes to ask you.

That must mean something to a girl
like you. I know a lot about sheep.
There is a great deal more to know.

C.J. Allen

Study for 'Francis Bacon (Drunk)'

Someone is asking, in French,
if he believes in God.

Non. Il n'existe pas.
So what does he believe in?

Beauty. The beauty of men.
He's rolling around, he can barely remain

upright. He's keeping on
the move to keep from falling

over. He has a glass in his hand.
(How many times have you seen him

without a glass in his hand?)
Does he go to galleries to look

at great paintings? Not much. No.
Well, he goes but he doesn't

spend long. He'll just stand
in front of a Rembrandt, say,

for a few moments then come away
with a violently

invigorated connection to life.
What's that hard light

in his eyes, concise
as a diamond? Shall we

open another bottle? Of course
we'll open another bottle. Now,

he fucking well hopes so, but
has everyone got what they want?

4

Alan Baker

Lying Together

Lying together we touch
fine skin & hair soft
as ships' calls on the fog-bound river
of my early days
of tidal surge
that bleeds both youth & age.

Lying together we touch
wood that all be well & the bairns
between us take their parts
& grow timely into them
as we have into those
we could not but choose.

Lying together we touch
the searching tongues
of yesterday that curl their flesh
to tell us in uncertain terms
that the gentle battles of the night
are over when we choose defeat.

Alan Baker

Once In Westerhope Workingmen's Club

much overtime and double-time was spent
in crisp notes, straight from the shift spent
scaling the sides of precarious ships.
Deal cards, order pints, bottles of broon,
twenty tabs and a box of dominoes,
and one for yourself bonny lad:
I supped it clearing smoke-wreathed
tables glass-stacked delicate replica
steelworks (long closed) seeing
welders, platers, fitters, apprentices
and bow-legged Walters and Arthurs
once ricketty children bent by labour, hearing
the barmaid scolding *'there's no need for language'*
as if there wasn't every need for language to ask:

what were they doing those hard-handed men,
drinking and playing dominoes
in the shadow of shipyards soon to be gone?
Didn't they know that time would come
no demarcation dispute could hold up,
no work-to-rule could win concessions from?

They did, as do we all, and yet
they loitered with intent
to drink their inexorable fill
and offer up each brokered advantage
to the drift of the river that ushered their ships
towards the salt-encrusted past,
to the barmaid calling time, to the overtime
and the double-time spent scaling
those towering, unsinkable ships.

Adrian Buckner

Slow Burn

Left out and yellowing by the lounger,
Culture from the weekend broadsheet:

the bearded middle aged columnist,
all chest, pocketed hands and brogues

stares out from his by-line,
finding more and more of life

less and less to his liking;
his words and gaze folded outwards

to slow burn, discolouring
with fertile spores of misanthropy.

At sundown the process is arrested —
words flap in the breeze

like the wasp, frantic for sweetness
the bottom of the glass.

Adrian Buckner

Cricket at Thrumpton

Lined up behind boundary flags
a fleet of Renault, Nissan and Ford;
only one or two from the village now
close enough to pedal or walk.

One of the old hands regrets the lack
nowadays of spectating wives and kids —
"Folk just don't have the time — always
something else they'll need or find to do."

The midday heat unfurls across a balmy
late afternoon — what fades for an hour or two
is the significance of change — absorbed
like tomorrow's heat into a reddening sky.

Long past the casting of the die, the game
ambles on without a trace of impatience;
courtesies are exchanged between men of sixteen
and sixty, a little light applause

for a manful effort at an impossible catch.
Something, eroding perhaps, is being passed on
as an unseen cow lumbers over to chew
the wing mirror of the fast bowler's Mondeo.

Wayne Burrows

A Recipe For Insanity

Imagine the earth as it spins through space,
so fast you'd panic if you felt it move.
You don't. Your feet are rooted, here.
Move them. See landscapes shift round you.

Speak. You'll make things come, and go.
It's easy: *The grass. The firework-burst.*
Think of a colour, any colour but red.
Instantly visualise: *lipgloss. Blood.*

Read: *...storms that scythe off rooftops*
start with the twitch of a butterfly's wings.
Tape talk shows, game shows. *News At Ten.*
Rewind them. Watch them again. Again.

Know language means nothing, in itself.
Signified, sign. It's arbitrary.
What you're saying's conditioned by habit, power:
The water's dark. The cat's on fire.

*Blackbirds are dinosaurs...*This is true.
Evolution. There's fossil proof.
They strut the earth as if they own it still,
croak feebly, mock you. Live on worms.

Take all this too literally, personally.
Mix in the contents of one day's news.
Leave to stand in the way you live.
Think deeply, continually. Fall in love.

Then eliminate prejudice, defences, lies,
take a concept like Justice. The ABC.
Read history. Let the contrasts brew.
Take a walk, look around. And think it through.

Wayne Burrows

Side-Effects

"...*wake now or never,*
For if thou nodd'st thou fall'st, and falling, fall forever"
FRANCIS QUARLES: *EMBLEMS* (1635)

That morning you were lying-in, stirring sometimes
in the turbulence of an overcast, late-April heat,
dreaming of entering a pharmacy, drinking a cup of
                                                    methadone
then rocking a lion to sleep in your arms
while stroking its mane in an olive-grove.
It's the anti-depressants, you start to explain that night,
they leave me so lethargic I can barely move...
You are weighing Serge Gainsbourg & Brigitte Bardot
against Stereolab's *Refried Ectoplasm,*
Bonnie & Clyde against *Harmonium,*
seeking something, anything, that might lift the mood.
It's so hard, you say, *to want to be awake*
when there's only work, this room and debt to be conscious
                                                    in...
You press POWER and PLAY, then set REPEAT.
I'm alright really, just a bit run down.
Tell me a story. Keep me entertained.
There's a joke about penguins you've heard before,
a 'twenties cocktail called an *'Angel's Tit'*.
You turn away, stare out over rooftops, yards, yet listen
                                                    hard,
follow the thoughts that slip unvoiced
behind the words I use. *It was strictly two-thirds cherry*
                                                    liqueur,
one-third cream with a cherry on top.
You'd drink it and think you'd seen the face of God.
Buttercups nod on a darkening lawn
and ivy slumps like a safety-net

in the shadows thrown by a carriage-lamp.
You tell me you're watching your own mind work from a
                                                long way off,
does that make sense, or are you going mad?
The orange upglare of the skyline burns
like rushlight on armoured, unmoving cloud.

Derrick Buttress

The Organ

Before his breakdown the boss played
methodist hymns on that old reed-organ
sulking in a grubby corner of the counting-house.
Each working day, when he went out,
I tried to force the lid, wanted to hear its voice
under the yellow keys. I ran the tip of my fingers
over the flowing tulips and swirling tendrils
carved into the instrument's dusty oak.

But he never played it now his god was gin.
He was cracking up in the inner sanctum of his office
He came out only to bawl at me for whistling jazz,
so I left it alone, as he left me alone
to guard the place when his gin ran out.
Alone with my imagination, still a kid at heart,
I played my games of private-eyes and cowboys.
I was Philip Marlowe and Buck Jones
sending evil into instant oblivion
with my smoking, two-fingered Colt.

Too lightly armed for rescuing the world,
I had my eye on the pistol-grip extinguisher
hanging by the door like a fat-barrelled gun.
Lifting it off its hooks, I shook it
for the sound of water, heard only a dry rattle,
and aimed it at the ceiling
with a delicate squeeze on the trigger.

What shot out after the heart-stopping bang
was not water, but a fine white cloud
of fuller's earth. It hung in the air
for a breathless second, then drifted down,
filled every cut and swirl of the organ's ornate pattern.
When I caught my breath
the instrument was an iced confection,
a wedding cake with candle-sticks,
an art nouveau adventure in white.

I rubbed and scrubbed, brushed and blew
in a panic rising to a sickness,
but I couldn't erase my crime.
My sacrilege was enough to tip the boss
into the black hole he had skirted for months.
I wept, wondered what lies I could tell my mother
when I got the sack, and had to face the music.

Derrick Buttress

Sealed with a Loving Kiss, 1944

My darling Will, I hope this finds you
as it leaves me — in the pink.

I don't go out much, as you requested —
just to Dolly's for a chat and a laugh.
Her brother, Frank, walks me home
through the blackout, right to my door.
He's turned into a nice young man.

Dad's busy with his leeks and onions.
Mam's pegging another rag rug.
Our Ron got the sack from Swann's
for swearing at the foreman.
Everything is just the same.

I went to the *Essoldo* the other night.
Saw a Bing Crosby flick with Doris Maplebeck.
Your old pal, Tommy Kew, sat next to me
halfway through. What a cheek!
He saw me home through the blackout.
I wish it had been you, my darling.
Remember our first date at the *Ritz*?
We saw *Now, Voyager*. You laughed when I cried

There's a new band at the *Palais* —
Sonny Gent and his Gentlemen.
So it's on with my glad rags come Friday night.
You know how much I love music.
If only we were together again
there'd be *You in my arms and a tear in my eye*.

14

Got to close now, my darling.
Mam wants the table for supper.
I will write again soon. Promise.
Dream about me as I will dream about you,
and please don't talk to Italian girls!

From your loving wife-to-be, Margie,
Till We Meet Again

P.S. Bob from next door has just popped in.
He's going to walk me through the blackout
to fetch fish and chips.
He looks quite smart as Brylcreem Boy.

Catherine Byron

This Was *Halal*

in a stone-built shed in Scotland
when the man with a licence to slaughter
lifted the five-month billy, all four hobbled limbs
and the asymmetrical ruminant body of him
into the metal wheelbarrow, so that his head
hung over the rod-rolled edge.
No ceremony of self-importance, just a quick
and single stroke with a blade.
And so he unlaced the carotid, and its small spurt, spurt
was what I caught, not entirely, in the
plastic bowl that I still have used, years since.
It was only afterwards that I asked 'So
no stunning, then?' 'I have to at work,' he said
'but I love to slaughter in peace, in a place like this
away from the smell of a thousand other deaths.'
Just the bleat of the kid, and of his brother outside
that had no inkling yet it was his turn next in the barrow.
'Look,' he said, holding his hands in the air,
'honest, I left the gun behind today. Won't tell, will you?'
Together we hauled the billy so that the last
fluids drained from its wound, and then he opened
another — the abdomen, sex to sternum. The packed case
    spilled
its ruffled whites and ambers and reds
into a bucket. I could make out the lights
as he wrenched them free. The liver. The heart.
'Ever want a job?' he asked as I finished
a quick swab down of the floor, of the splattered barrow.
I covered over the bowl and the bucket with empty plastic
    sacks.
There was no concealing the carcass.
'A job? Shall I fetch his brother?'
'Aye, we're as ready as can be.
Ever need a job, though, call me at the abattoir.
I pay good money to women. There's not many
has a call for it. Them that do
have a feel. They're the best gut-men I know.'

16

Catherine Byron

The Blue Darkness

I'm reading *Bavarian Gentians* and it's not death I see, or
    Persephone's shotgun marriage in the fields of Enna. No.

It's the long coarse throats of gentians gross as pitcher
    plants, lapped in the rangy grass of La Chartreuse.

Jos is wearing indigo jeans, Bavarian gentian jeans. His
    presence is marinading my innards to a soup. I lust
    luxuriously and on the quiet. He has no idea.

There are five of us on the valley road to La Chartreuse,
    down near the riverbed where the woodsorrel flowers
    are pale as shock, and forget-me-nots shake dull stars
    into the stream. Only the gentians hold the deep dye
    colourfast in their grassy spools.

A thin fire runs through my limbs. I am paler than woodland
    grass, paler than sorrel. I am seventeen.

Philip Callow

Home Ground

Early morning rain left little lakes
in the lanes and at the corners
of village streets. The air fragrant,
under a shrouded sky. The clop
of a horse still unfamiliar to him,
and he steps aside for the
massive animal, though there is
no need. The young horseman's rise
and fall asks to be envied
and admired. The road surface
freshly plastered with manure.
He is far off in thoughts,
but the satisfying odour in his nostrils
brings him back. In Somerset
he felt a borrower
but here he is native. It is
the Midlands after all.
Blackthorn in the hedgerows
explodes white smoke in clouds
with its last gasp.
Wood pigeons answer each other insanely.
A pheasant somewhere in a field
croaks like a mechanism in need of oil.

Philip Callow

Insouciance

The black cat deep in its fur
does not belong to us.
How good not to own animals.
He lies on the bed in the spare room
and raises a hind leg,
in the process of cleaning himself.
It is a leisurely matter.
While it happens he keeps one eye
on me, watching
in admiration from the doorway.
It could be effrontery
But it is sheer insouciance.
I close the door humbly
and then he miaows after me,
not desiring my presence
but wanting the door left open.
He is the master and I the mere man,
no doubt about it.

Malcolm Carson

Donaghadee

'A good Protestant sea, that,' said my cousin,
his face towards the Copelands
and the crack of early morning wind.
He dried the water from
his scaldy's neck to bloodless toes
with towel laundered barnacle-harsh.
An exile's son, still
I knew what he meant, could see
in the waves' swell and suck
the black flails of wrack
and thongweed that make
you kick out for the rocks
to clasp limpet-sure,
knees tucked to juddering chin;
could see the pools emptied of
the silliness of basking hours,
anemones now nipple hard.
And as I watched blood smudge
a delta from his chafed knee
I remembered the cacophony of families
— Strahans, Carsons, Craigs —
on ancestral picnics
in those Antrim coves,
and the English boy apart
in the rockpool's calm.

Malcolm Carson

Fish

1

Strange, they say, the feeling
first time you sink the knife
into the quivering belly,
slice upwards to gawping gills,
pull out guts, warm, still working,
then over the edge for gulls.
Some give an anaesthetic blow,
conscience's quibble.

2

As though out of Chardin
the cat is arched over sink and stove
insistent about the pan
of tongues and cheeks, gluey
in steam. On the slab
they were pearls of flesh
against the fillets' vulgarity.
Only purses of roe
could rival their discretion.

3

The kipper is by Picasso
each surface displayed
on a comb of bone,
fins relocated
to extremes, head
separated. Turn
it over though
and those eyes watch
from here, and there.

Peter Cash

Croft

Unfrequented roads run nowhere
except into one another. Even where they intersect,
signposts can only point forlornly
through flat pastures to the slow neglect

of All Saints' Church: a square
point of reference on which those doubts
— cast by open land and sky —
converge. Quite whereabouts

my ancestors had dwellings
(which made this tower imperative)
has — for this half-century, at least —
been hard to see: by 1965,

too few lived near enough the fete
to fill the Vicarage lawn again....
The closed school is an unused 'hall';
cow-parsley ruminates on Pinchbeck Lane.

In fact, I never found a churchyard
more confused, worse wrecked
— as if the community lost its shape
long before its last Searby died. In fact,

each grave is nothing but a clever stone
made stupid and illegible by rain;
nor can the table-tomb under the copper beech
— collapsed, embarrassed, vain —

be much of a comfort to Jobs
in their constant adjustments to loss.
Outnumbered children, with a dog,
rampage across the sunken moss.

Peter Cash

Ashby Puerorum

Why did they need another church here?
    What on earth for?
No sooner have we left Somersby
than this semi-undressed tower

pokes from a growth of sycamore.
    How come?
An unrhetorical sermon in stone
preached to a single farm?

Where did it take its text from?
    Despite its Latin name,
it's just another Ashby
which no antic features redeem.

No quoins for us to eulogise...
    Demographer, explain:
were there once *so* many worshippers
labouring up this ferny lane?

An impish Bishop was to blame
    — or so the farmer says.
He hypothecated its revenues
to keep his choirboys.

Stanley Cook

Rembrandt

My poems should be as sure, not flattering
For her whiteness any woman,
Nor favouring the mill child clattering
To early death, his thin legs swollen
Into clogs; but all things human
I should expose. No face has stolen
Importance from the clothes beneath
In work of his; but, as was true,
People he painted had the hands,
The hair and eyes to sorrow in,
The legs and faces for rejoicing,
Yet he forbade his heart to grieve
About some haycock huge old man,
Alone in the amber afternoon,
Or to be pleased with children playing
Whose knee backs dimpled as they ran.

Stanley Cook

My Father's People

In Gainsborough, South Kelsey, Morton and Scotter
The apple trees print a forgotten alphabet
On parchments of ground beside the inherited
Rosy brick of cottages and farms;
Streets made to measure horse and cart still serve
The shabby numbered gates of once busy works,
The unemployed that no longer dress up to sign on:
And I could panic that all my uncles and cousins
Who once worked here are dead, only alive
In flashes of anecdote from ageing widows.
For a family supposed to be fond of its stomach
That killed and hung its pigs and made one mouthful
Of cheesecakes and tarts they had indifferent health
Those connoisseurs of chitterlings and chines
Living on one lung and dying of ulcers.
Failing a poem, what else could they do but eat
The beautiful land I too find fascinating?
Poor writers, who gathered only at funerals
Or added to a Christmas card
"Mother died this June."

Andy Croft

My Favourite Martian

He stepped off a train from the wrong Cold War,
With crazy subtitles and a bad sound track,
Strapping the weight of half a world in his luggage,

Dressed for English weather like a mixed metaphor
And unpacking gifts tied, like tongues, with language.
But though he spoke in perfect syntax,

The local accents proved difficult at first:
He tried so hard to master 'unemployed' and 'duke',
Rolling his tongue round new ideas

Beyond belief, a lexicon of old English words
Comic and painful as onomatopoeias.
Lies are hard to translate, gobbledygook

For beginners, like brand-names, like Democracy.
Here every tongue's out on parole, life sentences
Of class, education, geography, precise as riddles,

Every helpful synonym another simile.
And meaning came whistling across from Mittel
Europa to fill those eager silences,

Like an international call with a two-second delay.
And then he left, and there I was, miming farewell,
Lost for words, watching the train pull out of the station,

Leaving us here so far apart, so far away,
And me so far from home, an alien,
Where everyone's pain has a different smell.

Andy Croft

Methuselah's Losers

A quick one-two, a turn, a screaming shot,
Back off the post, a run through the defence
To knock it straight back in, and though we've not
Yet touched the ball, we're one-nil down against
A team whose youth and energy subdues us
And makes us feel a bunch of hopeless losers.

Because Methuselah's too long to go
On Third Division league and fixture lists
We play as Losers and/or Meths — as though
We only lose because we're always pissed!
There's better teams than us made up of boozers,
And being sober's no help to the Losers.

At least we are consistent; losing streaks
Like ours take years and years of bloody training,
It's hard to be this bad, you need technique;
So please don't get me wrong, we're not complaining,
We don't think being useless helps excuse us,
It's just that practice makes us perfect losers!

You do not have to win to feel the buzz
Of sweat, testosterone and self-display;
Part circus show (including clowns like us),
Part theatre, part athletics, part ballet,
A game designed for gents that's played by bruisers
Who are long past their prime (just like Meths Losers)

Who, stuck in check-out queues and traffic lights
And meetings, still replay the games we've played
On Sunday mornings or on Wednesday nights,
The well-timed tackles, passes, goals we've made,
The unrecorded triumphs which enthuse us
Enough to turn out weekly for the Losers.

I like defeat, its sweaty, human smell,
Familiar as a much replayed own goal
Or spannered shot; this losing fits me well
(Just like our too-tight strip!) and on the whole
I think a winning sequence would confuse us,
At least you, know just where you are with losers.

While those who can afford it cheer success
Via satellite TV and sponsors' boxes,
On sweaty 5-a-side courts we transgress
The age's most unbending orthodoxies:
To be the worst! The thought somehow renews us:
Down with success! And up with all the losers!

Not coming first's an honourable aim
When winning is the only Good; there's pride
In coming last, in losing every game,
In being always on the losing side.
The games we really should have won accuse us:
Success belongs to others, not to losers.

Let's hear it then for those who're past their best;
Without us there would not be many winners,
We're here to make the numbers up, the Rest,
To teach the art of losing to beginners;
Their shiny, bright successes just amuse us,
For even winners have to play with losers.

So here's to hopeless losers everywhere
Who know we're stuffed before we even start,
Who live with disappointment and despair,
Who turn defeat into a kind of art;
An army of dissenters and refusers,
We'd change, the world — if we weren't such good losers!

Joan Downar

Grief as a Means of Growth

Crazy delphinium, blooming in November,
your favourite colour, violet-blue
like a southern sky or northern shadow.
I bring it indoors and it stands askew
in a vase and decides to shed some petals.
The house is shed of you,

and the larch that you planted's a russet hue,
another departure. I lie unclothed,
a madness of flesh in the muzzling sun.
How can I keep you? Grief unloads
strange fruits. I feel my breast
for the first floriferous node,

then stay my hand; always you over-rode
malignity with wit, were kind and decent;
you would not leave me such bequest. Bleak life
made glorious burgeonings, unexpected, lent
us joy, your gift which now amazed
I cull, unseasonal and magnificent.

Joan Downar

The Return of the Collared Doves

After the savage killings I missed them,
their misty maelstroms on the gravel
the portrait posing in the birch tree,
the soft utterings.

Then as you returned did they
— at least, a pair of them — a darker he
a blonde she, her back scalloped
like a tidal reach.

And I thought of the stuttering rhythm
of their blood, and how your heart galloped
under my hand and caught afraid
the offering of each.

Jeremy Duffield

Roake's Chandelier

I have read they are raising Roake's ship,
dragging it back from the grip of the waves
and ancient sands
beyond Trevose Head.

Perhaps your claim of seeing ghosts
in the mist where the sea and sky fused
half a lifetime ago
was not the Brocken Spectre I so lightly dismissed.

I still display the trinket of crystal;
it is an interesting conversation piece,
and now they say divers found the floor of Roake's cabin
scattered with the glass of his chandelier,

the one your family had manufactured for his last voyage,
but which we both knew
had been paid for with the blood of his black trade.
The facets of the crystal catch the light as I write.

Next summer I think I will walk that Cornish coast again,
pick shells, watch white-caps,
listen for Roake's laugh in the cry of the gull,
and your whispering in the spray of the waves.

Jeremy Duffield

Connections

Lifting a tobacco pouch from the open piano
I catch a key,
depress one note
bass and resonant,
sinister as a Hitchcock movie theme.

In black and white I see stairs and bannisters,
shadows along tall walls
and, out of camera-view,
hear a long, slow moan.

At one in the morning, returning home,
opening the garage door,
I hear a cow low in the allotment opposite,
a sound unnatural to prickle skin,
trigger scalp-tingle,
a shiver in the stomach;

and in black and white
and the darkness of trees and lawns
I listen for the crash through undergrowth
of charging buffalo.

Sue Dymoke

The Undertaking

No hope of telling him that day
though I had dressed for the occasion
dutch lace and cameo
velvet at my throat.

Absorbed in his experiment,
white bird flittering under domed glass,
he did not see the smiles
slipping across my lips,
sense the glimmer of yearning
in that shrouded room
dark save for the intense core
lamp and table gleaming,
him bathed in light
wrapt and uncertain about the undertaking
his girls in silhouette
anxious and wondering by turns.

No, there was no chance
for even the smallest sign:
I watched from the shadows
biding my time.

Sue Dymoke

Exhibit

Always semi-attentive, serious looking,
I've sized them up for hours, years.

Painters usually come and go:
Monet, Manet, Modigliani.
No trouble apart from the queues.
The impressionist crowd clucking,
clutching their souvenir tea towels,
tickets block-booked to beat the crush.
RA bloody RA.

That sensation shit was different.
Everything including the kitchen sink.
Bath too small for a decent dip.
House inside out. Inhospitable.
Chair sprinkled with pubes,

public staring, poking,
slipping themselves between slices of cow,
fruit-shaped body parts.
The pig's head gave me belly ache:
flies buzzing all day. Unclean.

Through sneers and smiles
they ignored me,
walkie talkie a distant murmur,
as they pulled faces at a quivering mirror.
Pug ugly.

Pacing I watched them
trace hands over hands
over hands over Myra.

Hung dung?
Just about the size of it.

Kevin Fegan

Undercurrents

A sandstone quarry lays the coastline bare
and bloody like a gutted salmon. Gulls
search for fresh fish and giant toadstools form
patio sets around a shaded tree.
Surfing t-shirts and bermuda shorts jog
along the coast road stopping only to
grab a crafty cigarette. A siren
warns of the incoming tide and public
notices list the things you cannot take
onto the sterile beach.

The mocking sand
blows against my skin and the sea sprays into
my face and I wonder what list of things
I will take off the beach. Sewer pipes aim
directly at the bay like cannons trained
against some foreign naval enemy
while undercurrents suggest that something
is happening just below the surface.

Kevin Fegan

Go West

Near the Mexican style church
on the border town of Barrow Island
there's a daily showdown in the DDH:
a siren signals the end for the journeyman
losing sleep and a week's wage
in a poker game in the double-bottom.

Men are spilling out of every building,
women race home with infants and shopping,
cyclists chaperon each other through town
while in the saloon bar at The Devonshire
two hired hands from out of town shoot pool
as shots of whiskey ricochet from stool to stool.

This is a wildwest town, a goldrush
boomtown at the edge of the sea
where labour is cheap and lives
are easily won and lost,
this is a frontier town
on the edge of its own prosperity.

Barrow, at the edge of the sea,
on the edge of its own prosperity:
land of the legendary goose barnacle
and scuff-resistant shoes, beauty queens, carnivals
and a few hometruths like a back-to-front town hall,
the upside-down sub., double-bottoms and 99 nightclubs,

iodine pills, chips and cheese,
marsh's sass and east german style cafes,
washing lines and lazy pigeons,
idle cranes and routine sirens,
the oyster catcher and the eider duck,
the sea dart, sea wolf and who gives a —

Rosie Garner

Home

So, where does she live now?
Not here, back in Pakistan
after nine years in England.

She remembers her wedding, how innocent they were.
He had to ask her her name, offered her sweets,
whispered that she should offer them back,
'Just to keep the old sticks happy.'
Something between them to remember,
sometimes it is nearly enough
to hang a marriage on.

Sometimes, in England, she could not breathe,
was dumb for days.

She thought she could slide back in.
She sits with her mother in a room
she remembers through her skin,
and she says nothing.

Every second day, she talks to her husband on the phone,
hears his voice loosen over the weeks.

She remembers how, last winter, he told her about
a woman who died of cold, alone on a mountain.
This woman, she forgot her compass, travelled north
instead of south, thought she was getting warmer
when all the time she was getting colder and so sleepy.

He told her this last winter in England,
that no one before had ever been
so tired or so cold.

Rosie Garner

The Thing Itself

Then there was that time last year when,
whilst looking for string, or when a tidy fit had seized her,
she opened the drawer and found daffodils growing in it.
This astonishing yellow filling her kitchen drawer
so that she could not shut it again without crushing stems,
trapping petals against metal runners.

It meant nothing.
Opening a drawer and finding dead bulbs flowering.
Not courage or desperation,
to grow like that in the dry dark.
The tenacity of life in the face of — not that.
Nor a metaphor for anything, a spider in a cave,
to grow like that in the dry dark where
a person might have said there was no hope.

One bulb had wizened and softened.
There was a faint dusting of mildew, barely a whiff.

It meant nothing.
Just this huge surprise and a vague feeling,
coming from nowhere,
that she'd been through this before.

David Gerard

The Hoop

He grasps the perfect circle
3-ply, re-cycling mirth.
A small boy's head,
Hair cropped, a smile
As wide as heaven
Framed by an entry's brickwork
Occupies this passage
In carefree rites of play.

The Wooden O will spin
Propelling him, young Mercury,
Past bins and backyards;
Sandalled feet
Won't stop at passage end.

One day, a lifetime hence,
Full circle,
Arm's length
Beyond a parent's care
To salvage him —
Re-entry.

Look homeward, youngster
Carefree still, in age.

David Gerard

Poem on His Birthday

Now
Is the familiar season,
Autumn in recession. Leaves
Abrade the failing days
Prodigal in russet,
Deep as the discounted years.

Later
Footsteps fade, dusk thickens,
Motion hangs through air,
Attenuated, bland, sublime,
(His native pale)
As, singly, days expire.
Where else can he tread
Thrashing damp leaves
Clotted like years about his feet
Masking all paths ahead.

The fall,
Treason's whelp
Turns summer last
Screws tight the heart,
Perverse, brings remaindered hours
To the brink.
Before next birthday,
Fast, too fast
Leaves the celebrant
To his bleak devotions
Naked on his plinth
While fades
This evening, yesterday, tomorrow,
Renegades.

Duncan Glen

Burned House

There's a burned house in the village.
A square upright house
on the hill next to the Library.
The brickwork looks very normal
but the roof tiles have gone
completely
and the rafters rise a criss-cross
of charred black
with patches of dull silver.
The windows and doors are boarded over
with brown plywood.

It's a dead man sat up
with pennies in his eyes.

Duncan Glen

Lords of Creation

Some did it in the beginning — of the Renaissance,
creating heaven and the earth
— in paint and stone and language.
And the world was with new form — and moved.

And Dante keeked owre ither Florentine waw.
See above the cypresses
towers and cupola
in the sky that red streak viewed in many a painting,

a skywalker before the reality seen seeming like
a creation of art. The renaissance painters taking
the tinted dust of the ground and breathing into oil paint
the breath of life, and each became a *living* god.

And these Lords of Creation said, in Attic order,
"Let us make God in our own image."

The image in head and heart, love and beauty;
together you hold and kindle
beyond time or place
with other fire, with other wings you move.

Not otherwise was Daedalus wakened
not otherwise was Venus born
not otherwise the sun that reveals heich and laich
light and shadow

naked stone and yirdly flesh.

On the sixth day the Lords of Creations
looked upon their work and saw
that it was good but not
good enough.

Daedalus unbound, as Michelangelo carves stone . . .
Venus rises from the sea, as Titian pents *colorito* . . .
Beatrice smiles as Dante scrieves beyond language . . .

The Lords of Creation spoke amongst themselves.
"Perhaps he divided the light too much from the darkness?"
"Perhaps he saw the light in the wrong light?"
"Perhaps he mixed the wrong dust?"

"That *could* not be!"

"Perhaps we need a new image?"

And God drew another breath
but did not waste it.

Cathy Grindrod

(At Newstead Abbey)
Taking Tea With Byron

Come back. Let this gentle greenness lure you —
the lovely thwack of cricket balls
beneath the elms. You could crack for me
that code of numbers I have never understood,
beside the old pavilion, taking English tea.

Bad to trample grass round ornamental flower beds.
Let's do it! Let's hide out in ivy-covered tunnels,
stir up the stew pond, vault monastic walls,
startle swans beside the lake with manic yells,
shoot antlers off the stags' heads in the hall.

You considered lobster salad and champagne
the only fitting viands for my sex. You'll learn.
For a while, I'll acquiesce — I, in my petticoats, at home,
as we eat supper here, beneath this Japanese pagoda.
Flick of pithy orange peel; coy carp, white stone.

And now I'll tempt you to a weeping willow's shade,
lie with you, hidden at its swaying core, while peacocks keen,
yawp-yowling from their turrets to the dark drop below,
grieving for unfinished pasts, or creaking out a warning cry:
Beware! Beware! She may be dangerous to know.

Cathy Grindrod

Exposure

Tie knotted even to tea; suits, sentences
from sample books; today, my father wears
a T-shirt, arms worm pink, hairs pale
as a red-head's eyelashes. Once only,
shirt removed to mow the lawn, heat
lashing his tender back to sun-stroke and delirium,
did his words make no sense. Now
his lips stick wax-white at the corners
as he smiles, distressed; complains of cold.

Underneath one arm, the utter shock
of this; a white rope twist; strong
as a tuber root — stitched in; gathered
top to bottom, like a button badly sewn.
I have never never known. Exposed,
he has to tell of being twelve, a Scout
in short sleeves, running, skating, sliding
on the parquet of a school gymnasium floor,
heading for a plate glass window,

knowing that he could not stop, and running.
Sliced into his pale skin, the thing now aches
like him, for touching. I think I know
how that might be — the way my own arm
aches to feel itself around him — curved,
tied, solid as a braid. Stubbornly, it stays,
like him, locked by my side. Instead,
I offer him a cardigan; one he can
fasten later, should the need arise.

Madge Hales

Swans

This was our Spring ritual, up the
Reclaimed lawn to see the swans, ducks,
En famille again, but totally unprepared

For what we saw — survival of the fittest:
The pen swan, seven cygnets, six sturdy
Made the frail one more noticeable.

Watching we became aware of this one
Striving to claim a ride on the mother's
Back but each time she, the mother, with a

Heave of her great wing, shook it off.
Horrified we became fixed: incredulous.
Four times we saw it happen, shrunk now

To a grey rag. We knew we watched it die.
Yet could not believe it. We humans who
Cherish our weakest were feeling sick —

The fourth time it did not surface.
Then the whole family swam serenely on.
We were quiet over tea trying not to think

Of a truth that appalled us, as mothers.
For some days we ignored the river, kept to
The garden. The water had lost its lovers;

We had been right about those cold-black eyes
And saved no bread or left-overs of cake. Even
Leda's swan would leave us cold that summer.

Madge Hales

Wrong

It was wrong; not natural as seasons are,
snowdrop to michaelmas. Buds hardened
browned by frost never to flower. It was
always on the books but grammar was a
subject missed through childish illnesses.

That first bedroom, married — though
accepted unquestioningly was a mean room,
narrow bedded but cheap at the price like
me. After it was infants so there was no
time to speculate being wordless, tired.

It was wrong since the age gap and the rape
war brings; he knowingly took a man's
advantage. At least the pay was almost nil,
housekeeper, whore if passive, a place to put
up for the night. Now he has departed, old,

lusty to the last: gone. He never saw I was
me that last decade — someone was — his
ever ready angels were there, paid in full.
Being left penniless seemed natural in the
circumstances. Tainted perhaps, the money.

It was wrong now it is over. The wardrobe,
drawers, cloakroom, to the rag-man for free
secret boxes unlooked in, to clang the dust-
bin lid on; war trophies to make a splash
in the Grantham canal where the lawn ends.

Arms, doors, windows wide to all who thrive
on air: the fetid smells that thrived here
the filth, bleeds out. Time that breeds patience
will, one day, lay a ghost of gross dimensions.
The end was the beginning never had —

John Harvey

Driven By Rain
After reading Tess Gallagher's 'Amplitude'

And when finally I look up, lost,
from this book, I'm shocked
by the sudden wash of rain
that blows in swathes along this slow
suburban street I'm trying to call home.
So strange, the way it can be there from nowhere,
filling out your world, everything you see: memory.

That day we climbed almost to the summit of Cadillac,
so hot you went skinny-dipping in the lake
while I sat propped against hard rock,
drank from our thermos and read,
only stopping when you emerged, glistening and ready,
eager to make the most of our time, the weather ...
And then, when we clambered, exhausted,
over the last broad grey stones,
the sky, from nowhere, black with thunder,
those first stabs of lightning fixing the peaks
opposite and closer by the second, so that,
yards only short of the summit, we turned
and ran, laughing with panic, leaping over rocks,
newly wet and slippery with rain, never losing our footing,
me clinging to your hand as if my life depended upon it,
which of course it did.

John Harvey

Apples

My father is dying.
Scent of apples from the night stand.
I reach out my hand and rest
one hard against my face;
he taught me how to tell the real thing
from the fake; hold it close beside the ear
and shake — a genuine Cox, the seeds
will rattle loose inside their case.
You see. He told me
and I swallowed every word by rote.
Five cotton towns of Lancashire,
five woollen towns, four rivers
that flow into the Wash — Witham,
Welland, Nen and Great Ouse.
Once learned, never forgotten.

My father is dying.
He died nine years ago this June.
They phoned from the hospital
with the news. His face a cask
once used for storing living things.
A cup of tea, grown cold and orange
on the stand beside the bed.
Length of his fingers, nails like horn,
unclipped. Though dead,
my father is still dying,
oh, slowly, sure and slow as the long fall of rain.
I reach out again for the apple
and bite into its flesh
and hold him — bright and sharp,
safe inside the hollow of my mouth.

Keith Howden

Air Men

This is that golden England. Always in black and white.
These are its mythic villages, their never streets always
striped zebra by an always sun, high summer's ever habitat.
And they await you here: the irascible but finally all-right
blimp Colonel, the Rector smirking his rose garden praise,
the garrulous Postman, old maids with boudicca bicycles
whose heron profiles hide a softened heart. And always,
   the *threat*

that lived in wartime cinemas where dust and V sign fingers
garbled the moonshine's passage to the screen. There too
was the Control Tower, alert, ceaselessly sleepless
to guard against the *threat* haunting that seamless
enclosure of azure sky acquired by this *Meccano*
and *Hornby* world. And here, maintaining for you
its own brand of sunlight, is lush grass with summers

of flowers blatant or covert, undyingly profuse
in propaganda fields. Listen: the domestic insects buzz
the industrious drone of their trades. In such a universe,
bees blur to hymn and celebrate the absolutes
of land lying loam and rich, whose pastoral and friendly trees
adapt their limbs to patriotic gestures.
In their untroubled shade, a modest Church is

pointing a Heaven that only these trees, these villages,
these people deserve and own. Yet *threat* is somewhere.
For here, horatian on the foreground grass
are the young men, the devil-may-care freelances
of the sky's regions. Artless, they breathe a purer air
than those among the dusty seats reading the atmosphere
redolent with *threat* impending as the structures

50

of an Auden poem. These are the paladins in sheepskin armour
whose exhaust trails bulletin the empyrean,
scrawling their love affair with death, whose youthful clamour
blazons just cause. Some lounge in deck-chairs. Another
writes his last letter to a winsome girl. An idyll's reign
is always too good to last. Even in cloudless skies, the obscene
must lie concealed where air already holds the echo

whose dangerous meaning clatters in the klaxon
calling to arms. Mess doorways explode. There is
that galvanising rush of the young knights, at a run
pulling their flying-suits to shape, with laughter hauling on
protective leathers and stirring to war-cry the dull fuss
of trailing thongs, the snick and clash of harness
that marks their sunlit scramble. Here starts that
　mythical mission

to win the grail, to stem the waste-land's inroads.
Spitfires and *Hurricanes* wait a tarmac for ever golden,
where an English sun anthems on England's fields,
gilds English trees, pulpits its hallowing trades
on the stones of an English Church. They squadron
to serve such never icons, that never congregation
of winsome girls, of Colonels, Rectors, Postmen, Old Maids.

Keith Howden

Dynamo

The wind is in the east and icy.
It is six months since Hitler died,
five since VE day, four since the explosion
that scoured Hiroshima and three
since Attlee ousted Churchill. Droning blurred
in grey November, a lease-lend Dakota,
wings bannering the red star's sign
steers into Northolt's landing area.

Thirty nine Russians dubiously descend
to the wet tarmac: then the taciturn
interpreter that the press christens
Alexandra the Silent. An east wind
is blowing. Not long ago, Stalin
condemned Prokofiev for the formal
intricacy of his style. '*Do Russians
need sheets?*' is the question at the Hotel.

For fourteen thousand pounds, Chelsea
sign Tommy Lawton. Five shilling tickets
tout for a fiver. The east wind's rain
soaks Ration Books in a bomb-scarred city.
A few journalists in grandstand seats
chatter dismissively, are unimpressed
by Russian training. Recently, in
East Prussia, Solzhenitsyn was arrested.

'Chelsea will sweep them off their feet.'
'Completely ordinary,' is the headline
in the Sunday Express. *'Don't expect poise*
from factory hands. Lawton will get
a hatful.' 'Chelsea will easily maintain
our football supremacy,' avows
the People's columnist. *'These pale boys*
are far too slow.' An east wind still blows.

There is a collective gasp. The Russian
eleven shuffles from sweatsuits and disports
the Dynamo colours. A dark blue strip
thrusts a pink D on breasts blustering in
a cold east wind. Their long blue shorts,
unusually, are bordered with white bands
and emerald green socks twist at the top
to white on these pale factory hands.

Worse seems to follow when each Russian
presents a large and colourful bouquet
to his opposite number. It has the scent
of dalliance, or worse, propitiation.
The crowd droops dumbly at such unmanly
happenings, then gorges on chauvinist
gloatings and jeers. Only the sentient
see pennants flapping a cold wind from the east.

What happens is the unexpected:
inch-perfect passes from these hacks,
a new athleticism and such slick tactical
awareness, such spectacularly fluid
movement that leaves the English backs,
unused to such adroitness and precision,
looking bewildered. Stalin might well
condemn such intricate perfection.

Later, touring the blackened city,
they make their official visit to the grave
of Marx in Highgate, salute, though shopping's
still on the agenda. And eerily,
the rationed world feels less safe.
Sleet spits the tarmac where a plane,
a Dakota with red stars on its wings,
blurs out of Northolt. An east wind sets in.

Pamela Lewis

La Mère

The sea washed the sand
smooth as a good mattress.
Waves drew up the beach
as though invisible hands
were making up beds.
Breaking waves mimicked
the crochet on my mother's
many trousseau sheets,
I looked for her monogram,
large white curly L's.
I have some old music.
Looking it out I shall find
Elgar and Debussy and will hear
the sound of the sea again
and remember waking as a child
to hear her playing the piano.

Pamela Lewis

Motherhood Considered on May Day

Damn fertility,
woman is a maypole.
  Children dance
    every day of the year
  holding bright ribbons.
The intricate ritual
is measured on mothers.
  Sometimes the pole
    is patterned
  with satin.
On other days
sad bands become entangled.
  Ribbons lengthen
    as children grow,
  the dancing is less frequent.
Ribbons hang limp
for days and weeks,
  taken up on festive days
    and woven
  into a holiday.
Sometimes reins
become bindings,
  black armbands,
    soiled and torn mementoes
  of spring innocence.
Some maypoles stand for a lifetime,
tended and well-painted.
  Others fall, lie unregarded,
    are left to the ravages
  of winter.

John Lucas

An Irregular Ode on the Retirement
of Derek Randall, Cricketer
for Ben

My Batter at the bridge, tun-voice-and-booted Randall,
who in presumptuous youth once chose to long-man-handle
Shuttleworth, Lever and Simmons — Lancs' gruff and
    grudging trio —
and won for Notts a match they'd hoped to draw. *Con Brio*
at the non-striker's end Great Garfield Sobers stood
to grin applause at cover drives that in due season would
drive Lillee so distracted he'd steeple at your head,
though "no use aiming there, mate, there's nowt in it,"
    you said,

"try pitching 'em up." He did. And your Centenary
innings flowed, a two days' binge, golden, crisp and buttery.
Yet oh, what homecoming waited on that wondrous 174:
Your Trent Bridge Test, and run out by that uncallipygian bore
Boycott. But then a county game at his own Headingley,
he prods to cover, sets off, and the "coiled cobra" he
had not considered zaps him with wit, speed, grace,
those Son-of-a-Gunn gifts you poured into summer's space.

All shirt tail, pads skew-whiff, slewed cap and Grock's
    slumped walk,
"The Sun Has Got His Hat On" you'd mourn or scatter talk
wide as fielders, bat parsing each ball in optative
mode: "I choose to cut or pull, to sweep or glance or drive,"
while stripe-tied types snuffed gin, muttering "Crackers
in one's opinion. Chap's not one of Us." True! And Packer's
Circus couldn't corral you, nor did you make bold
with Greig, Gooch and Gatting to stuff your boots with
    randgold,

but once again Down Under upped to bemused Brearley:
"Only ten minutes more, Skip, it'll be fifteen to tea";
and, care thus summoned, dispensed with care three plush
    fours
to hoist your hundred, sink Hogg, and become fit cause
of Arlott's measured words: "He made the method men look
    sad."
And so you did, and such sweet madness had spectators glad
hand you to pavilions, who knew the back-page scandal:
you were too rare a player for England, dear Derek Randall.

John Lucas

Reading Ovid in Beeston

Geranium red is not the red of blood,
so how come that as each new petal fell
and splashed the grass, it could have been a sigh
like breeze-filled branches I heard well
up from the ground beneath this flawless sky.

Drowsing, I thought the bird that dropped the seed,
translated from Africa to England's May,
had lifted it from an Aegean island
where, scythed and spread to sun, the dead plant lay
as though prepared for some ambiguous garland.

Trying to rewind change can do no good,
but now I spooled from petal back to a girl
emerging from Saronic blue, then, seized
in a taloned grip, limbs flailing, and the swirl
of waters as she's plunged to deepest grief.

Later, thrown clear, she's buried in a wood
By herdsmen, desperate to hide
the guilt of gods who killed because they could.
And then the flowers come up from her grave,
geraniums, red as guilt, and spread worldwide.

Julie Lumsden

Staying Awake for the Results — Polling Day, 2005

Post democracy, where do we go from here?
We wander down to throw away our votes.

These days I'm either out of it by nine
or trawling the channels for serial killers at midnight.

Comedy is good. Whole series played back to back through
the small hours. The Third Reich never fails to engage.

During the breaks, I take peeks down the road where
   nothing happens.
Frog ring-tone, Peel Mask, some rock star telling me to
   worry about

Veronique, bright scarf wound round and round her head;
her belly, a full high moon —

all the women, everywhere, praying for nothing more
than to sit awake among the smooth sleepers of a
   quiet house.

I'm not a bad person. I wouldn't put cattle in cattle trucks.
I drum my nails on the windowsill. Sigh.

Julie Lumsden

Skegness and Global Warming

The Fun Fair and the concrete fort;
Lisa loves Liam, fading with him
inside a thin green heart, next to a swastika
and *shit* and *Sarah is a slag*. All waiting
for the triumphant sea.

Clare MacDonald Shaw

Novice

A body in the bath – it wakes and stares at me
from a quilt. This house is thick with flesh;
armchairs have coupled up in the hallway,
bedding nephews down for the feast.

Jeanne's ironing hangs from prints; old bishops,
foxed by flowering damp raise hands, eyes,
in cloth gardens, deploring their chipped gilt.
She pities my cold land, summers without wine.

Madame's at the station, picking up aunts.
Jeanne drags out glass-crates I'm not to touch.
A chef hired with the silver invades her kitchen.
While she counts spoons, he flaunts *bouchées*

all chicken-scented morning. Upstairs stinks
of smoke-bomb; their factory waste breeds flies
in rusty ponds. Pierre lobs dozens at lunch; his dog
eats the dead, out of courtesy, between thrown bones.

Madame returns. Blackest swathes and hat
set off silk wings uncreasing from the Citroën.
Is it the fiancée? *Mais non!* Why did she run out
last night? Will she be back? I'm sent to the terrace,

where Mlle Lamarche sits by laurel tubs
playing patience with the wind; I fetch hearts
and jacks from gravel. Pierre, behind me, closes in.
No cause for alarm, though — married, at least forty.

He shrugs, joins the massing guests. We sit
on iron lace, looking out. She's spent her life here,
distant cousin, loose thread in the fringe; her brother
died young, *là-bas*, down in their factory.

(Was he... caught in a machine? One does not ask.)
A taxi! Voices go speeding up; this is the great return.
Photographers shoo us away, reading omens of light.
Blood-kin burst doors, flow down steps, congeal
  for albums.

Mlle Lamarche will not face the shutter; she is against
all this. Even so, she would have given the bracelet, but
it was taken, it was lost: *mes topazes*... Half-told tales —
asides to a foreign schoolgirl — stick in the brain,

splinters from crossing lives. She bares her wrist at me,
showing the mapped palm. We are called to table;
flies skate over gum lakes of aspic, multiply in sauces.
Jeanne has a bowl of insect eyes, black seed-pearl,

sticky eggs; she fishes up for each of us
spoonfuls of emptied sea. On a raft, burning,
losing sight of islands, I shall drift and starve it out.
Or try the caviar, warily.

Clare MacDonald Shaw

Blue Fever

As centuries end, blue fever strikes. Decadents
caught it last time, from Liberty Japanese;
now dredged-up Nanking at Harrods

inflames collective nerves. Anything cobalt on china
is suddenly more visible, as *House Style*
promotes undustably fragile shrines to sapphire.

(Readers, in the grey decade slipping towards the noughts,
be comforted with icons of summer. Catch
sky-melt in our plates, scoop the sea.)

Mud-bed cargoes sell legend: pirates, hurricane breakers,
the deep sucking. Through reigns, revolutions, fish
gaped at themselves, jellied in ultramarine; salt tea
    slopped in bowls.

In more advanced stages of delirium,
you need a great mantel, baroque,
for the electric dazzle of K'ang-hsi, or Ming mei-p'ing,

and they'll be alien. You understand
a crane, a phoenix, can guess at plum bloom
from cracked-ice Christmas ginger-jars,

but pearls in flames? borders of gongs and fungus?
Looks like a foreign zodiac, needs deciphering.
Our holy symbols — lilies, lambs, Catherine wheels —

flew down to infant heads from Sunday windows.
Virgins, we know, like to wear blue stained glass,
but Chinese scribbles for clouds don't signal fertility.

Later shipments make easier reading.
In sampans, stick-fishers float above pines;
teahouse or temple, the pavilion's familiar,

though English potters have yet to draw
the winning blueprint — lovers, bridge, catkins. Their cups
diluted the rum East to everyone's satisfaction.

More curious, from tombs, not water: rough provincial ware
— peonies burst through compost, cracking glaze —
  empires ago
sent south to the fringe of Asia, where fever was endemic,

where thin pots sang celestially,
struck in gamelan music, or shielded
the precious parts of the dead — earth to keep earth
  from earth.

Here, now, the diseased collector
strokes the cold bellies of jars, shivers, recalls
celadon fakes in the shed, the crash in etchings.

Out East, fine vessels, broken, served as pieces for games.

Jamie McKendrick

Home Thoughts

The airmail from India, a weatherbeaten blue,
with wax marks from the candle you had used
to write by reached me. You write that reach
is what travellers there do rather than arrive
being more respectful to the gods of place.
For years your letters from around the world
have kept on reaching me wherever
I'm hunched beside an atlas and a lamp.
When you last saw me I was living in a room
across the road from but a floor below
the room we used to share ten years ago.
Only kindness stopped you saying
it took me quite some time to cross that road;
and looking from my window I expect to see
myself looking out to where in ten years time
I'll be looking back again to see... the last things
you mention are the Parsee towers of silence
where the dead are left for vultures to attend.
I warm to that. It sort of brings things home.

Jamie McKendrick

Banana Boat

'I wasn't born on a banana boat yesterday'
the porter told us (not that we'd asked)
when we tried to bluff our way without a pass
into the Liverpool University Pool.
He growled then waved us through the turnstyle
with a wink as good as a season ticket.
Did he know me from somewhere, or just think he did?

As for me, I wasn't born in a bungalow.
I was, come to think of it — not so much born
as put together, the main piece fitting into place
when we moved to a house above the Mersey
and the concrete rampart of Garston Docks,
the barbed-wire and the pill-box from the war
— the main piece, or so I'd like to think.

But if Pat Cassidy wasn't born, as he said
he wasn't, on one of Fyffe's banana boats
which from the Albert Dock used to supply
the whole country with bananas (except during the war)
that didn't rule out he might have been born
on some other boat like a vessel stacked
with iron-bound trunks of Swedish pine

on their way to be axed into matchsticks
at Bryant & May's factory down the road,
or in the hold of a ship from Trinidad
full of sugar cane for Tate & Lyle's.
Certainly there was something
scouse-maritime about him — an old hulk
moored to a sandbank on the river.

He made me think of the one heirloom I had
(from my mother's father I'd never met) —
a Bermuda-rig model yacht plank-built
by Mr Rawlinson, his friend, the docker,
and of the foghorns' shindy on New Year's Eve
when the boat-lights blazed at the stroke of twelve
where Sassoon had dumped his Military Cross.

Still, whether on one or another sort of boat,
at sea or in dry dock, no one would dispute
that Corporal Cassidy, who had (I found out)
served beside my father in the Second,
admittedly, and not the First World War
no one would dispute he wasn't born yesterday
though his cheeks were as pink as if he was.

Stanley Middleton

I Hear the Vitali Chaconne

There was ground bass, some autumn tune
Edged with a silver figure, swathed in sky,
As living as that dead Vitali, unknown
Son of his father, could emboss. To die
Like that, to resurrect
Wide, universal space in a quiet room
Must be ambition, body sprung erect
To purpose, doom
Delivered. The chairs, the paling walls
Books lavishly bespatter, and the slim
Hand easing her violin.
Hold me. Let me not break so, Lord, din
Into my ears an apathy. I cannot bear, I will
Not bear that beauty; it has killed all
My richest learning.
String for string moves, a silver facing
Friezed on a marble bass. Model me not,
Vitali, mould me not. She sways,
Faintly American, to sacrifice herself
To herself, like Othin strung nine nights
On a windy tree.

There are dreams there, counted on fingers,
Few as that, but real, life
Of no fardels, painted with no strife,
Players, singers,
In an idyll, time unspanned.
What noise is that? Of hand to hand
But rough dream-awakening, clapping as they
Rush out to stay
Them with flagons. May
They, even they, recall the fine-filed form,
The dominating fingers and the wide
World of Vitali, carved upon the air
In these four walls, lavish with ghosts
As autumn's drawing near.

Stanley Middleton

Epiphany in the Schoolroom

Some thirty serious boys potter at books;
Tall windows chatter as a dapple of rain
Teases the yard, and thirty noiseless clicks
At nerve-ends in the cortex mean

That grave eyes, blue, grey, brown, stare up;
Owners begin to mutter, point or ask
Involved, half-wistful questions. I stop
This short. All's sheltered once more, brisk.

I measure the delighted moment's scope,
Now a ghost scrape of pens, and cross a thought
That sets me pacing aisles, gives me the slip
Out of this classroom world, yet closed in it.

Blake Morrison

Grange Boy

Horse-chestnuts thudded to the lawn each autumn.
Their spiked husks were like medieval clubs,
Porcupines, unexploded shells. But if
You waited long enough they gave themselves up —
Brown pups, a cow opening its sad eye,
The shine of the dining-room table.

We were famous for horse-chestnuts. Boys
From the milltown would ring at our door asking
Could they gather conkers and I'd to tell them
Only from the ground — no stick-throwing.
I watched from the casement as they wandered
In shadow, trousers crammed like mint-jars.

One morning they began without asking.
Plain as pikestaffs, their hurled sticks filleted
Whole branches, the air filled like a pillowfight
With rebellion and leaves. I was alone.
I had not father's booming voice. They were free
To trample through our peaceable estate.

Afterwards, matching father in a show
Of indignation *(bloody vandals and thugs)*
I imagined their home ground: the flagged backyards,
The forbidden alleys and passages
Winding up and out on purple moor,
The coal-sacks glistening in locked sheds.

It is June now, the chestnut scattered
Like confetti. He summoned me today
To the billiard-room — that incident
With an apprentice. *I've told you before.*
A son in your father's firm, you're looked to
For an example. I don't know what to do.

72

So I sit at my rosewood desk, lines fading
Across the parkland. I've been getting pamphlets
In a plain brown envelope and feel like
A traitor. Strangers have been seen
By the wicket-gate. Mother keeps to her bed.
English, we hoard our secrets to the end.

Blake Morrison

The Kiss

His Buick was too wide and didn't slow,
our wing-mirrors kissing in a Suffolk lane,
no sweat, not worth the exchange of addresses.

High from the rainchecking satellites
our island's like a gun set on a table,
still smoking, waiting to be loaded again.

Graham Mort

Storm Larks

Sky is black as a ciné film spooling its last
reel; imageless, burned by the light, its
white-gashed celluloid flickers overhead.

The horizons tremble, then stand still,
accepting the warm rain; our breathing falters,
uncertain as purple in the sun's fading bruise.

This frequency is all wow and flutter and rumble
on the earth's slow platter, its grindstone
flinting out split-second streaks of light.

The gleam across your face fixes it here:
white, ecstatic with shushed exclamations —
then bass notes beginning below hearing's octaves.

It's ironic we don't think of God now, only
of the ions colliding, those fronts of heated air
and copper dousing-rods drinking an electric blue.

But it's death-sky music, you said so,
your hand on mine glimpsed as a claw of bones,
so old it could be winged or scaled, half-human.

Lightning fuses air's nitrogen, cattle stumble
awash in curdled milk; ponies' eyes panic,
their mouths foaming at rain's polished bit.

The voltage goes to ground, missing the uncoiled helix
of acids that wash away, futile for a billion years
until the chance of it lights like a struck match.

We're sheltering by this gable-end, watching
the town blitzed to monochrome, seeing skylarks stall
then fly on singing into the air's stunned height.

Graham Mort

Geese from a Timber House

That summer house. Its veranda and pitch-
pine frame, cracked windows, slant walls,
shot-up carpet straddling the stairs,
the smell of damp and pre-war family
holidays still seasoning each room.

Long days: reading, writing, watching the tide
trying to tear away the beach, rearing where
scores of geese steered south before the gales.
All over England rivers overflowed, the
railways had packed up and you were

travelling towards me, stranded on a train
with no real notion where I was. A borrowed
beach-house, that's all. The cuffs of my jumper
catching at a page, a coffee pot branding the table
like the thought of you, that we'd be together

and everything alright again, despite
those gales, the flypast of geese foretelling
worse to come. I wandered by each window,
hearing tiny shrieks of wind, watching
bushes tear their hair, and felt alive

with loneliness, wanting to mark a vee of
kisses in that favourite place behind your knee.
Then you rang and I was gunning the car
through floods to meet you at Saxmundham —
that fly-speck dotted on the map.

Night dropped. Tracks glittered into rain.
The train came late. Each mile of B road to
the coast was fraught with wind, high water,
fallen trees; then village lights shrank the dark
and I was opening our door into a stale

summer-scented past. We slept in its memory,
woke to calmer seas, to geese planing waves,
landrovers braked in the road, serious men
gathered in Wellingtons and woollen hats,
their fingers stroking walnut stocks.

We sidled through them for our walk,
trudged two miles through spray and shingle,
deafened by the sea. It was later, hunched over
whisky macs, the gas-fire drying our shoes,
we heard the guns begin to talk.

Peter Mortimer

The Old

Don't ask about the old days
Don't let them grow misty-eyed
about cobbled streets
bone shaker trams, doodle bugs
ration cards, squeaking mangles
Reckitts Blue, or that outside loo.
Don't gather them to sing the
Flanagan & Allen
they remember from crackling bakelites.

Memory has made husks of them.

Let them talk of tomorrow
and what is to be done.
Because the next sun to rise
though it may be their last sun
is one hundred times brighter
than every sun already set.

Peter Mortimer

Sausages

What do they dream of
as they wheeze and whine in the pan?
Why so restless? They shift
and roll, this way and that
defying our intentions
for their all-over tan.
Or sometimes they explode
split open like old settees
a grotesque spilling of innards.
Other times, through a tiny blowhole
they send up a thin fountain of fat.

We want to spear them onto the plate
but they resist; will not come quietly.
Though we have forced them through a machine
though butchers have twisted them to shape
like a clown squeaking balloons
they bulge and strain; a size 18 in a tight dress
a condom swollen with excitement.
And to remind us, sometimes, they send
a sudden Exocet of fat direct into the eye.

Michael Murphy

Elsewhere

Do you remember burying the thrush
we found laid out stiff on the cinder track
beside the railway; perfect as a mammoth
swaddled in a coat of soil and permafrost,
how you wrapped him in a Kleenex
among broken pots, split canes and bulbs
sprouting in the loamy darkness
under your dad's shed?
                All night,
at opposite ends of the city, we waited
to see if — if — feathers, beak and all the
intricately coiled stuff

had, with morning, ascended.

Michael Murphy

Morning Song

Heat-struck, I lie awake
imagining a body where there's none:
you, your heavy limbs at rest
beside me in our Welsh-pine bed
back home, and almost catch
the sound your breathing makes,
withdrawing, an ocean to the north.

Here, behind the old town,
a scooter gears up past the cypresses,
hot from a moonlit assignation.
Stars over the cemetery wall,
silent breakages of fire,
go down in the restless sky.
Bougainvillaea rehearses its torch song.

An hour from now
and the sun will start to climb
inch by slow inch
through the resinous pine,
fishing boats strung out across the bay
will rewind their nets and I'll re-play the words

you slipped into my case:
  I'll be dreaming of you
  when you read this.
So, for now, let silence alone
make inroads into night,
sifting the world for a sound
I can hold, as a shell, to my ear,

permitting each rigorous thing —
in-itself — the soughing tide,
wind in the trees —
to arrange themselves as bluntly as
light reorders sheets,
the precise blurring the matter-of
fact: dawn and its homesick ghosts.

Henry Normal

Experiments with Worms

Cut them in two
Just above the thigh
And humans do not reproduce
Both halves die

Prove this yourself
Take a human from the shelf

Now here we have a vivisectionist
Some question the workings of this
So in order to dispel doubt
Earlier I cut this one's heart out

Still we're keeping it breathing
On a cigarette machine
No need to be squeamish
It's clinically clean
And the end
Will justify the means

Vivisectionists have no feelings
Spray perfume in its eyes
Sure it cries, but it never dies
Here have a try

We've got to be cruel to be kind
And we just may find
Some medical advance
And sometimes by chance
You can be cutting up a specimen
And suddenly from the mess there in
You can make a great achievement
So we're all in agreement
We can feed tubes into his brain
And record the scale of pain

As we burn acid through his face
It's for the good of the race
Let's make this world a better place.

Henry Normal

The Last Poem I Ever Wrote

The last poem I ever wrote I had such high hopes for.

The last poem I ever wrote was to have been so powerful it would make war obsolete and nuclear fusion as vital as trainspotting. It was to have been so cleverly constructed it would hold the key to the very universe itself, make Arthur C. Clarke redundant and James Burke intelligible; so full of life it would be strapped onto wounds, and made into tablets and ointment. The Olympic committee would disqualify competitors found to have read it. Laid over the face of a child's corpse it would bring the dead back to life.

The last poem I ever wrote was published in a low budget poetry magazine boasting a print run of 220, 150 of which still remain under the editor's bed. The title escapes me but it was some pathetic pun such as "Write Now."

The last poem I ever wrote was performed to an alternative cabaret audience at Cleethorpes off-season in between an alternative juggler and a 22-piece Catalonian dance band. Coinciding with the call for last orders it was heckled constantly by a drunk born and bred in London who sang in a scotch accent and claimed to own the city of Glasgow personally.

The last poem I ever wrote was entered in a poetry competition by a lifelong enemy. The judges having been certified dead were suitably appointed as their names were unknown even to each other let alone to anyone else. My poem came 63rd out of 7 million entries and won a year's subscription to the Crumpsall Poetry Appreciation Society Crochet Circle and Glee Club Gazette.

The last poem I ever wrote was cremated along with my body, unread.

The last poem I ever wrote was carried in the hearts of those I loved.

Betty Parvin

Gulls Aground

In the green harbour muck, the gulls
All smooth as sea-pearled mussels search
For succulent stuff. Strung out in the weed
Some strut, some loll on the slip
And a lone one limps about.
The yearlings croak and the old
Stand around with gossip and laughter,
Lazily shift, or stir their stumps in the rot.
Far off, where the small boats lift,
The sun's edge severs the knot.

When food is found they suddenly have no truck
With each other but, flurrying after,
Will steal, strike, tear and shock
With crude claw or clattering beak
The bird with the luck,
Jerk the crab from its jaw, chop,
Joggle and suck the scrabbling stark
Shell creature whole into their own maw.

White-eyed they watch for the ones who will come
To throw crumbs and crackling crusts
For the nimble to catch on the air,
Scramble and snatch, give slow, soul-freezing call,
Swoop, slide stiff-legged, tangle again and go
Down to the glimmering slime in a white-fanned fall,
Till the wind-drift turns, the weeds congeal and flow,
The visitors shiver and turn their backs on the dusk
As the tide licks in; then gulls alight in a row,
Form up, and glare like ghosts from the lime-washed wall.

Betty Parvin

Tortuous Chinesis

Penderus the poet dined with his rivals in the
house of the Caesars where he often went hungry

For Envio the steward who served them at table
was a vain man and his enemy.

In consequence of this his rivals grew lazy
and clogged with oil and their verses likewise.

While Penderus stayed agile and fresh, his
appetite sensitive and his verses likewise.

The people acclaimed him, the Emperor heard him
and rewarded him lavishly.

Out of his wisdom, Penderus presented his enemy
with a rich farm deep in the country

Where Envio, bored with the social inadequacies
of nature, son dined and wined himself to death.

Tom Paulin

A New Society

It's easy enough to regret them when they're gone.
Beds creaked on boards in the brick meadows
Somewhere above a tired earth no one had seen
Since Arkwright became a street name.

Their boxed rooms were papered with generations,
There were gas lamps, corner shops that smelt of wrapped
    bread,
Worn thresholds warmed by the sun and kids playing ball
Near the odd, black, Ford Popular.

Then they were empty like plague streets, their doors barred
And windows zinced. Dead lids weighted with coins,
Dead ends all of them when their families left.
Then broken terraces carried away in skips.

A man squints down a theodolite, others stretch white tapes
Over the humped soil or dig trenches that are like useful
    graves.
Diesel combusts as yellow bulldozers push earth
With their shields. Piledrivers thud on opened ground.

Just watching this — the laid-out streets, the mixers
Churning cement, the new bricks rising on their
    foundations —
Makes me want to believe in some undoctrinaire
Statement of what should be. A factual idealism.

A mummified Bentham should flourish in this soil
And unfold an order that's unaggressively civilian,
Where taps gush water into stainless sinks
And there's a smell of fresh paint in sunlit kitchens.

Where rats are destroyed and crawlies discouraged,
Where the Law is glimpsed on occasional traffic duties
And the streets are friendly with surprise recognitions.
Where, besides these, there's a visible water

That lets the sun dazzle on Bank Holidays, and where kids
Can paddle safely. There should be some grass, too,
And the chance of an unremarkable privacy,
A vegetable silence there for the taking.

Tom Paulin

Under a Roof

It'll piss all evening now. From next door
The usual man and woman stuff rants on, then fades;
And I know she'll soon be moaning, climbing her little
   register
Of ecstasy till quiet settles back like dust,
Like rain, among shadows without furniture.

There was a mattress on bare floorboards when I came,
But now I own a bed, a table, and a chair
In a house where no one knows each other's name,
A zone where gardens overgrow and privet rankles
It stinks in summer and it blinds the panes.

Cats wail at night among the weeds and bricks,
Prowl rusted fire-escapes that lose themselves
In hedges turned to scrub. Exile in the sticks
Is where I've ended up, under wet slates
Where gas flames dry the air and the meter clicks.

The girl I had scared easily. She saw
The dead bareness of the floor, her body near
Both it and mine, so dressed and left the raw,
Rough room I'd brought her to. Up here I'm free
And know a type of power, a certain kind of law.

Noises, the smell of meals, the sounds that bodies make,
All reach me here, drifting from other rooms.
And what I know is how much longer it will take
For thoughts and love to change themselves from these
Than rain and rooms to find their senseless lake.

Nigel Pickard

Joke

So you attempt to tell a joke
involving two cowboys (who, necessarily
in this instance, are non-gender specific,
but of their own cultural-historical moment
all the same) and one Red Indian.
The latter, though the cowhands' dialogue
is informed by the basic tenets of realism
posited within Propp's traditional
narrative framework, we decide
ought to be a Native American,
even when referred to by either of
the egoless ideological constructs
of that particular and paradigmatic
site of struggle notionally called the United States.

So you attempt to tell the joke, but then
someone questions whether one of
the indigenous population of those parts
would've followed two cowpokes
on her/his own; and isn't this, it's mooted,
inscribing a predatory, not to say
homogenised view of multiple cultures
intrinsically localised
and diverse? Thus you (wo)manfully
struggle on through further objections
which may or may not be relevant; and, as it
turns out, the punch-line is quite funny
in that crap kind of way.

Nigel Pickard

Being a Man

You walk behind
the bearer
who carries
the tiny box
your baby boys are
both lying in,
and I'm staggered
that you manage
it. One foot
then the other,
moving,
like that. And
at the edge of
the grave, you
hold your wife
to stop her
being swallowed
too, while small
children from
the neighbouring
primary school
spill out to play.
I find myself
having to
look away:
at the fields that
light and wind
scour, like time's
speeded up;
at the other
mourners, who
look equally in
the right and wrong

direction, though
no direction — this
way or that — feels
anywhere
like secure. Except
afterwards, in
the pub, you are
there again,
still upright,
holding
your wife, saying
you know where
they are, that's the
thing, that's
the main thing;
somehow certain,
still somehow
making sense.

Peter Porter

Addio Senza Rancor

'Such past and reticence!' — George MacBeth

Two girls in their last year at school,
in the back row since they are taller,
stay young in the autograph album
which has slipped into sight from among
the fallen contents of the bookcase. Here, are
the ingredients of sorrow, forever renewing
itself by generations — one was to die
at forty-one and the other at forty-four.

Not young by the standards of the world's unfairness,
only by those of our spoiled corner of it.
Why do we go on manufacturing misery,
waking when it cries, cleaning it for school,
clapping at the prize giving? The new girls
are in their mothers' clothes and the new fathers
stripping for the shining theatre instruments —
Unhappiness lives on, depression dies early.

Friends and lovers, kept apart by photographs,
we have made so much life to give away,
our generous faces must outlast us!
The shadows of that richness look over
my shoulder as I pick up a postcard
with a bent pin through it. Earliest yellow leaves
are appearing on the plane trees in the square —
the playground of maturity shall bury them.

Two friends high on death — what can I say to you,
not having experienced the mystery
which choked you? Nothing of the ordinariness
which lives in words and pictures trained you
for such priesthood. You are nowhere
in the evening light: what I see instead
are two white presences, playing with life,
smiling and letting it go without reproach.

Peter Porter

Good Vibes
For Shena Mackay

If you hadn't noticed the unprominent sign
We'd have missed Adlestrop, missed the gone
Railway and the bullock raking his back
In the hollow holly-bower. Missed, too, the sky
So intolerably lofty in its beakered blue
And the loping dog which frightened me
(Which is how I know he was friendly) —
Most noticeably missed the station bench
And ADLESTROP, the railway sign, with Edward
Thomas's poem on a plaque for pilgrims.
Not a great poem, but rich in names
And heartache and certainly a focus for
A sinisterly fine October afternoon.
Down one lane adjacent the Home for Children,
(With what impediment we never found),
All the day-labourers of Oxfordshire and Gloucestershire
Were about their honey-making masonry
Of Cotswold stone, and the bullocks were nifty
In the meadow by the creek. There were no
Devils in the landscape, exhalations from
Ponds and dogs' breath and graveyards after rain
Could only be imagined in such unexpected sunshine,
But we felt them, felt a new humidity,
Oppressive like the self. This was a short halt
On two pilgrimages, a look-back out of Hades,
Such as the gods provide for laughter in their Chronicles.
Yet that sound, that risible division,
Strikes mortal earth some otherwise — such as
Gravel flicking from a low-slung bumper,
A trailing jet above, a jostling on the eaves
Of sycamores. It was as if the well-intentioned
Dead were breathing out and blessing everyone,

Vibrations of the minute, without franchise,
A pointless benediction. Thinking again, I feel
Grateful that you saw through uncleaned windows
A name which meant the same to all half-educated
Persons. To have trod on ground in happiness
Is to be shaken by the true immortals.

Allan Rodway

Nunhead Cemetery, Peckham

Silent. It is a dying place,
this once-thriving terminus.
Like the last Romans
its regular guards have gone
leaving the grave and cryptic dead,
huddled behind stone shields
hidden in dungeons, defenceless,
to fend for themselves.

Now, the great necropolis crumbles,
the forces of invading nature
swarm over all defences,
sacking the sanctuaries, harrying
houses of the inoffensive dead,
fighting over the spoils of peace,
rudely putting every body to life.

Glide by those tree-rent gatehouses
blinded by brambles, sinking
open-mouthed in a green sea,
slip through the Sleeping-Beauty overgrowth
to where a vista'd church looms legendary,
pick your way past fallen masonry
beneath the ivied Gothic porch
to read, minute upon the mighty door:
  Warning — keep well away.
  Grave danger of collapse.

Well away, gravely endangered indeed,
the grey, standing army does collapse
rank by rank by rank vegetation defeated.
Clawed down by climbing creepers
(as stiff grey eminencies tend to be),
by tree-shoots shattered, battered by trunks,
hauled under, netted by grass-roots: routed...
though doomed platoons, cut off; still stand
shoulder to shoulder in glades' green glooms,
some staggering headstones, near an unachievable
Way Out, support their stricken comrades still,
and still some upstart messages get through:
    'Jesus wants me for a sunbeam'
(Poor Mary Ellen, aged 64, a shade among such shades!),
    'The world's most perfect husband' —
sadly dissipated now... Only Great-War graves,
trim and smart in well-drilled squads,
preserve a sweet decorum, 'pro patria' —
protected by what mercenary band? Their
memory *shall* 'not perish from the earth',
just yet, though all who knew them have.

But see that hard-won clearing there — how Death
fights back, struggling for *unlebensraum*! —
where two upstanding sepulchres fend off
the bark-clad vandal giants' with fiery flowers.
And lo! shining on the final treeless verge
a bright new grave is born. Naively hopeful:

Life lets no-one 'rest in peace' for long.

Go back, while go you can, to London's roar.
Grave cities have gone underground before.

Allan Rodway

Time and Tide

Creeping up, the tide
Has thieved my very footprints!
And where's my life gone?

Peter Sansom

Peach

The peach is not a political animal.
You can pack it in a crate and load a truck
if you're careful: a peach bursts easily,
and a little consideration pays dividends.
Ship it properly, and warehouse it, wholesale it,
and then at the point of sale
for the sideboard or flan, or even pulped for yoghurt,
then, when all's said and done, you can say
the peach was meant for this. Dumb, and not of course
any sort of animal. The downy flesh
is seeing a metaphor by touch. And what's more,
it's bought and paid for. It's not anything like us.

Peter Sansom

Sheffield by Night

After the nightclubs have turned out and before
the cleaners have plugged in, the city is as still
as a snowglobe this last day of summer.
I sweat up Paradise St that was Workhouse Rd
and out under green-lit trees of the cathedral
like strolling through an artist's impression;
then over new tramtracks that dad would know
as far as the Cutler's Hall and HSBC.
A dog walking itself in the corner of my eye
past Pollards is gone before I see it's a fox.
Next, Boots the Chemists bright as a cruise ship
but the Marie Celeste; then over Fargate
and down Chapel Walk, the Link, the Samaritans,
and double-take at shoes a month's wages;
past the delivery-end of M&S now turn left
by the Crucible. I'm not mugged
in the subway or offered sex to feed a habit.
Ghost roadworks on the steep bit of Flat Street
and in the waking Interchange Paul Simon's
got that ticket still for his destination.
The Grade II listed eyesore on the skyline
is a memory of the Socialist Republic
and in its people-centred daring typical
of Sheaf Field, home of the cyclepath and bendi-
bus, the most wooded city in Europe if you
don't listen to Brum, and the most parks too,
that turned the steelworks into a shopping centre,
and the shopping centre into another world —
then suddenly here, at what I think of as Midland Station,
to carry this lightheaded flu to Nottingham.

Vernon Scannell

Autobiographical Note

Beeston, the place, near Nottingham:
We lived there for three years or so.
Each Saturday at two-o'clock
We queued up for the matinée,
All the kids for streets around
With snotty noses, giant caps,
Cut down coats and heavy boots,
The natural enemies of cops
And schoolteachers. Profane and hoarse
We scrambled, yelled and fought until
The Picture Palace opened up
And we, like Hamelin children, forced
Our bony way into the hall.
That much is easy to recall;
Also the reek of chewing-gum,
Gob-stoppers and liquorice,
But of the flickering myths themselves
Not much remains. The hero was
A milky wide-brimmed hat, a shape
Astride the arched white stallion;
The villain's horse and hat were black.
Disbelief did not exist
And laundered virtue always won
With quicker gun and harder fist,
And all of us applauded it.
Yet I remember moments when
In solitude I'd find myself
Brooding on the sooty man,
The bristling villain, who could move
Imagination in a way
The well-shaved hero never could,
And even warm the nervous heart
With something oddly close to love.

Vernon Scannell

A Numinous Event

Only once in my life have I experienced
A numinous event. God spoke to me.
I do not mean this metaphorically
Or by dream or through Urim or a prophet
But that He spoke to me with a physical voice
Which issued from the mystery beyond
The dark sky and its white rash of stars
On a frosty night on Ealing Broadway.
I stood transfixed, amazed, my face raised
To feel a silvery beatitude descend.

I don't remember the exact words uttered
Nor could I honestly describe the voice
Except that I would swear that it was male.
But this I do recall with total certainty:
The tone was benevolent and reassuring.
Church bells began to roll and tremble in the skies
For it was Christmas Eve and all the pubs
Had extensions of their licences.

I think God was forgiving me for my absence
From His mass. I know that He spoke to me,
Although the words themselves are lost
Or, if not lost, are hidden in the mist
Of almost half a century. And yes,
I must confess,
I might have been at least a little pissed.

Alan Sillitoe

Lancaster

At twenty-two he was an older man,
Done sixty raids and dropped 500 tons on target
Or near enough. Come for a ride, son:
Hi-di-hi and ho-di-ho, war over and be going soon.
He opened a map and showed the side that mattered,
Thumbed a line from Syerston to Harwell.

Our bomber shouldered up the runway
Cut the silver Trent in May:
Three years in factories
Made a decade out of each twelve-month,
From the cockpit viewing Southwell Minster
Under a continent of candyfloss,
Fields wheatened green recalling
Chaff blown and remaining corn
To soften in my sweetheart's mouth,
Then into a hedge and crush the dockleaves into greensmear.

The pilot banked his hundred wingspan south:
How much magnetic, how much true, how much compass —
Work the variation through,
Two hundred miles an hour and a following wind,
Harder to get home again over lace of roads and lanes
Plus or minus deviation for a course to steer
Red and black on spread map at the navigator's table,
A smell for life of petrol, peardrops and rexine.
Run a pencil down from A to B —
Now on the fortieth anniversary I reinvigorate
The game which formed my life's dead reckoning
Impossible to fathom as in that bomber I assumed I could —

Everything mechanical and easy to work,
Map in top-left pocket, crawling the long coffin
Between bomb racks and centre section
No view of the world for forty feet,
Parachute forgotten but who goes back
At seventeen? Who thinks the air is not for him,
Merlin engines all his own, strip map beckoning
Through Death's cathedral for a dwarf?
Everything is there to open: the rear gunner's turret
For a technicolor backward view
A track made good of woods and the botch of Leicester
Railways of Rugby, the sandstone of Oxford
The peace of Abingdon and first view of the Thames,
Canals and rivers of new reality, calico tablecloth
Hiding all in me, unseen from my chosen seat.

Better not to know how I reached the far-back turret
Of downdraught and upcurrents, eyes on the past's
Wide fan shaping my destination.
A button put me side-on to the slipstream,
An east-west variation of the view. People ignored
The buzzing of our passage, engines hiding the silence
Of a so-far buried life, looking over four guns
Ready to suck all spirits up like fishes to a net.

Cherish the distance between them and me
But get inside the theatre of what goes on,
Or open the door and tumble into space —
No one would know I'd gone or where, destroying
The homely panorama and my body.
Death would not burn the spirit but I'd be off
And out of the map, shoes, tunic and cap looted
By gravity: Hello! as I spin, so glad to know you
But I never will. There, I don't belong,
My place forever looking down and in.

Alone, far back, to face the vanishing horizon squarely on.
Dim as it is, don't go, corrupted by haze
Loving what I cannot reach. The theatre's anatomy
And madness missed, don't care about a full cast waiting
To come in order of appearance and perform their dreams,
Ambition's engine, curtains holding back
Till the planet Lancaster divides the space
And I return over empty bombracks to get born again.

Alan Sillitoe

Oxney

Smoke all evening, too thin
to move. Stubble aflame
Up a hillside when I drove
Across the flat half-mile between

Iden and the Isle of Oxney. A line
Of white, lipped in red, set a corner
Of the battlefield on fire,
And cloud like a grey cloak was pulled along

By some heart-broken mourner going home.

Sheila Smith

Bank Holiday on the Nottingham–Beeston Canal

No coal, or iron, or trudging horses
but Slim No 1, uptight, from Chichester Basin,
registered in Waterford. Curtains twitched together.

Liquorice black, brass like trumpets,
a foaming head of geraniums — barges
anchored nose to tail at the canal's edge.

'Narrow Escape' strictly functional. Maroon and silver.
Shipshape and Nottingham fashion. A sharp dog keeps
watch from its inexplicable home.

Marine guernseys confer on Killarney and Brum.
The towpath gives room to impromptu lidos
disrupting the Saturday column of shoppers.

Trawling through cans in duckweed pools
a clockwork coot forages for her young
except the one she kills, sickly, not worth the feed.

Mallards buck and toss in the wake unzipped
by the blue launch heading for the lock,
its windows flat with frightened faces.

Youth at the prow, going the other way,
are triumphant, just miss an old working barge,
bloodied with rust, no cabin, decks furred like sacking.

Unlike the others, it stays. On festivity's edge.
Sometimes, unseen, it moves its mooring. No birds land on it.
A bull elephant claiming its space.

Sheila Smith

Fading Out

There was a grey cat in the Beat Hotel
Numéro 9 rue Git-le-Coeur
where Lies-the -Heart. Madame Rachou
ran the Beat Hotel for thirty years.

Mirtaud the grey cat fell
from an upper floor window.
He survived. But used up
one of his nine lives.

Ginsberg came and went.
Bill Burroughs assembled
a Naked Lunch, with help
from his many friends.

Brion Gysin dreamt up,
created his Dream Machine,
built images from the flickering mind.
Gregory Corso was sick on the stairs,

wrote 'The Happy Birthday of Death'.
When the rest drifted away
he lorded it, 'The Poet' in Paris,
a cape, women, a silver-topped cane.

In '63 Burroughs watched
the Beat Hotel die.
'It was owned by Madame... she moved
sort of across the street. She looked
so sad... like people... when they retire.
She had geraniums and an old grey chin
and an old old grey cat...
she just faded out.'
He might have been wrong.
She might just have rented it...

(With acknowledgment to Barry Miles, 'The Beat Hotel,
Ginsberg, Burroughs and Corso in Paris 1957-1963', Atlantic
Books, London, 2001)

Mahendra Solanki

Always There

Your idea for keeping us safe
is for us all to sleep together,
huddled against your ghosts
in a room paid for in advance.

You would keep us fed;
cooker balanced in the corner,
food stored in the oven.

We would stay indoors.
School, work and love,
unnecessary distractions.

We would never grow old.
Strangers, you tell us,
would only lie.

Mahendra Solanki

"If it be love indeed, tell me how much"
for Hannah

You say, "I don't love you,"
pinching your forefinger and thumb,
your hand a small fish's head,
"even *this* much."

Arching both arms out, you say,
your arms now a seagull's wings,
"I love David *that* much"

At five you think of love
as a measuring rod;
each notch a fist
to use as a bargaining tool.

On your first birthday, I thought
of time as a measure of love:
a life-time of love a year old;
"I'll love you for ever" held at the water's edge.

You and I stand on a shoreline.
We are bound by what we hear and say.
Stones sink like hopes.

How can I gauge the depth
of the sea we throw pebbles in?

Michael Standen

Last

Someone mentioned it, a last
To mend shoes on, 'an iron thing
With three different feet, you know', she said.
I did. I knew the very thing, but long removed;
I only had it with me as a ghost,
A wartime memory from being very small,
The wonder of a father's allowed skills
To keep the family dry-shod in the war.
It sprang to me, an anchor sort of thing
With three black feet of differing size,
Three witchlike feet allowing him to mend
Whatever kept us going then.
And with the mention of the last came back for me
The waiting presence of the past,
Something you sense validity
Gathers about although you know it does not,
Has nothing to say, no clear-cut point,
No general word to any other...
Except you say yes, wait a minute,
For me yes that brings back something,
It brings back... I know exactly what you mean.
Three black feet, heavy, made of iron.
I've got one somewhere but the one I've got
Mends nothing but my sense of time.

Michael Standen

What Eng. Lit. Did For Me

Where red Nottingham brickwork was
on Berridge Road great towers stand.
The Council packs them in, except at meetings.
That road was packed with Chaucer then as I,
incredible now as any of his May mornings,
woke to find his lines between the bricks
pointing that street towards delicious literature:
my Middle Ages
lay like dew on kicked schoolbooks' pages.

We were the last lot ushered through
portals dusted by the British Council.
The revolutionary T.S. Eliot
was still in residence and much relief
that the New World gold rang
to old standards was in the air:
they nursed their old scars and Isherwoods
and gave a cordial, if muted, reception.

A year before in a sunny school library,
a choice group of spirits — the master of the VIth
(unsymbolic Essex fly drowsing the volumes)
sorted him out syllable by polysyllable
with rich good humour and interest unfeigned
(to borrow as he did occasional cadences).
His despair unfolded as from a pyramid
'the curse of modern life', we were not cursed
but trusted this intellectual version of the news
we'd been brought up on: rationing and war.

Pyramids for us yielded British goods,
almost exports as Attlee's clement gown
sheltered the sprouts of understanding and the sun
set round the globe in fading pink
which did not blush for us; it was just
what we expected: it was just.

116

Martin Stannard

Danish Pastry Girlfriend

If you're planning to jump out a
Window pick a low one; if you're planning
To run in front of a bus pick

A slow one. If you're planning to jump
In a river pick a dry one; if you're planning
To jump off a bridge don't

Pick a high one. If you're planning to open
A vein pick a Please don't continue this,
She said, it's alarming and tasteless and it's

Not poetry. But it's about survival, I said,
And she blew a smoke ring at me and my head
Disappeared although she had given up

Smoking and I had also given up smoking
Because smoking can seriously damage
The things you bought. And it's not

About survival, she said, at all. It was
At this point I realised I didn't want to
Have a serious conversation with

Anyone so I went and got myself a Danish
And here is where I say Pastry or Girlfriend
But I don't know which one's the one.

Martin Stannard

Whelm

Underwhelmed is as vital a critical reaction
As over. Equanimity: perhaps the meaning should
Be clarified before I go on. This morning Ivy

On the sill is looking more dark-edged, Rose
Upon the table is past her best but they are both
And always will be beautiful girls. The flags

In the kitchen are softening with age; with age
Perhaps with flags may one begin to establish
Dominion? If I knew what I was muttering about

I would expect you to answer the question
But it's okay: continue to smoke your bonfire
And I will continue to bring you twigs

To wrap around your thing in place of my arms.
Once upon a time I just couldn't get enough of
You but now I have had more than enough of you;

Do you get it? The gift of plain speaking comes
And goes as does the courage of my convictions,
Confidence in my abilities, strength of purpose

And what is this? Oh, Lily is drooping in
The drawing room and in its cage a little bird —
Ennui — is looking pretty kind of disinterested

In these on-goings. There are issues here
But no answers; it is okay to say that; I don't care
If you don't like me any more; it's an opinion;

The outlook from the window is undulating
Because of the hills. I am not sure anyone can
Describe what they don't do for me and mean:

I mean: Is there a God of Flowers? A God of Love?
Is there any way in which an ordinary person with
Good intentions can just be untroubled and whelmed?

Jenny Swann

The Discus Thrower

I turn in at the gates of the British Museum
for refuge from the rain, and thread through statuary
in bronze and stone, to where Myron's famed *Diskobolos*
looks down on us,

the veins on his cold, white thighs raised in smooth relief,
his perfect body clenched to send the discus spinning
into a blue, Athens sky (I watch it soar over the gasps
of the crowd, hold my breath to see where it lands).

His inner balance would fill me with wonder and envy,
his flawless beauty seem a cruel reminder
of how our own strength slips,
our mortal dreams fall short,

our hopes drop to ground,
were it not that as I stand here, humbled,
in the hush and echo of polished marble,
I notice his head's on the wrong way round.

Jenny Swann

Bread and Butter Pudding

I pour milk, sugar and beaten eggs
on the buttered bread, leave the pudding to swell
in its dish on the sill

as the dairy float drones down the hill
towards my open front door
with its fringe of waving mallows,

jasmine trailing over the trellis,
a robin pitching songs like quoits
into this lazy summer morning's idyll.

Then the sun goes in
and the burble of background radio voices
slides into focus —

there's no unhearing
how, elsewhere in the world today,
on the wrong side of a fence, a town, a war,

women are dragged out of dark-windowed houses,
their soft tongues slit,
their scarved heads clubbed.

My bread and butter pudding sits
in its dish, soaks up
sugar, milk, eggs, blood.

Deborah Tyler-Bennett

Nottingham Evening Post, Valentine's Day, 1914

Fifty lines on how King George may visit
the Duke of Portland and attend the hunt,
and thirty on a bride-to-be named Blisset
whose name on marriage will be Lady Blunt.
Twelve for stories full of postcard humour,
someone in Beeston swallowed her false teeth,
a window-cleaner caught a glimpse of bloomer
and was mistaken for a petty thief.
Another fifty-one detailing billiards,
a further thirty on the boxing ring,
or fancy dress with courtiers dressed as Hilliards,
and ten on hats that are the latest thing.
Four on great grandad, working at his stall,
killed at just thirty-six by pit roof fall.

Deborah Tyler-Bennett

Letter From The Road

Wilf,

We're at a heavy weather place, and no mistake,
rain's whip lashing us without a break,
our tent roof burst like unset jelly,
wet punters called for returned pennies
(we didn't laugh, we didn't laugh at all).
Remember two week ago? You and I stood in thrall
of honeyed fields, thinking how summer was near done.
Now, brother, it seems we never had one.
   Dank hosses steam, but we move tomorrow
no point in grooming. Well now,
are you wintering at Mansfield? If you are I may just see
   you there,
but first we have the autumn round to look to — Goose Fair,
Loughborough, then the Lammas. Lately
I'm bare knuckling again, you know no man can take me,
I dare say you'll be much the same. Finn painted a new booth
(Robin-red and gold) showing us all rosy. I'm loath
to say yours truly looks bozz-eyed.
If it don't leak, that booth'll be a forrard stride.

Brother, I think that's all. Except to say,
a certain girl's been asking of you. May
you prosper, she said, and begged to tell
the linnet as you bought her's doing well,
singing like it had freedom. Mr Bardon suffers, looks
unlike to last the winter. That'll be another old one off
 the books.
He coughs all night, wheezy as a bad accordion, so grim
I wish I couldn't hear — even rain don't muffle him.
If I don't see you afore I'll meet you at the Lammas,
 and bring
a certain linnet's lady. Till then she'll be fortune-telling
and I'll take all comers, the best of English youth,
bare knuckling in Finn's Robin-redbreast booth.

Your ever-loving Bro',
Jacko

Hugh Underhill

Fallen Nature

Ah, what shall language do?
JAMES THOMSON, *THE SEASONS*

Two crows on a football pitch. Their beaks
whack at anything, an empty Walker's Crisps
for instance. Fog-nuzzled trees

attempt hieratic presence. December's
strutting its stuff
as months do, in ordered sequence, and with names,

which are but how we speak them:
whatever disarray the world's in, they get
extralinguistically on with things, like the zig-

zagging ducks and always overwrought
kerfuffling geese
here where yellowed willows

issue dripping bulletins —
news from nowhere (though one knows the text)
of what fixedly recurs, immanent, ineluctable etcetera,

over against the balls-ups *people* make?
No, these car foglights can probe as much as they like,
they won't find anything except the way we speak of
   things —

what we magnify, our love's transfigurations,
and then that ever-mutant disarray, that huge dismay
thumbing its nose at our avid brilliant language-games.

Hugh Underhill

Blake's Cottage

In my aunt's house were many mansions.
She let them out to summer visitors
who from her garden gate let out themselves
on grassy foreshore, café, beach huts, shingle

that picked the trembling light off rumpled sea
to spatter the air with 'particles bright'
which Blake in eighteen-hundred limned
as tall emanations, prophets, poets.

These glided now past residents with dogs
which sniffed enquiringly at unseen heels;
prickled our flummoxed guests with feather-breaths
as they staked their transient claims and boggled
at pooled life on tide-frisked sands —
the art of mini-crabs to melt as mud
and shrimplets' backwards-leap alacrity.

The family foregathered there for roomy
Christmasses, with Gran well cossetted
against the drafts, for all the balm
of 'Felpham's Vale'.
            Summer usurped
the dining-room for guests, for us the kitchen's bounds.
We smashed the waters with our back-strokes, crawls;
skins turned salt, burned swart.
                 Blake
said in Lambeth was a grain of sand that Satan
could not find. I thought I knew of such another
five minutes from his Felpham thatch

his 'roof of rusted gold'
just on from the *Fox* where he had rowed
with Private Scofield. I was in my days of longing.
O when would its ravishment descend again,
Los's fiery whirlwind

126

which had there set William down at the long, low,
clematis-garnished cottage
behind packed walls of Sussex flint? I swear
I saw one of his angels once

paddle, as over Botticelli's stable, up on that thatch.
I had my dreams. I would drown in the air, sound
with the pines athwart the flinted wall, catch fire
with blazings of sun on the windows.

The bus into town
shambled through the village past buff-brown walls
and protrusion of turret, a feint of fairytale
bewildering my childhood. Hayley's place — he
who went sailing off horses, an open umbrella
for spread canvas, and had put in a word with Los
to bring William to Sussex.

Other worlds called,
Carnaby Street a-swinging, and around its corner
I chanced on the spot where William was born. Only
years on did I make the tube-pilgrimage

to the S.E.1 site of his Herculean labours:
in that hero's road, he sang of little girls lost,
hopelessly asylumed, yards from his door. His token
here's a plaque on trim brick, and this PCV-
U double-glazed in brilliant white
estate inherits from him its address. I know

these day I know no angels emanations spirits
yet *now* I'll swear he's here in more than name,
mansioned in this air, those walls.
Keep at it, good old friend: pity's
in short supply, and still, in our latter age,
minds are their own jailers.

Eddie Wainwright

Bearding the Bard

When you've come in after a hard day at the cutting edge,
all you want to do is tweak a few bottoms, pull a few pigtails,
get pissed, feed your face, and kip. Night after night, slumped
     over
your dinosaur stew, just as the mead was beginning to do its
     stuff,
there was this twangling at the front and the tearing sound of
     some idiot
who seemed he'd been at the Capstan Full Strength for
     decades,
clearing his pipes before boring on. And then it went on
and bloody on: warriors hacked off at the knees, dragons,
biographies of everybody's sententious old grandads (who
     were
invariably good blokes and shining role models, declared
the twangling idiot). Reassuring in a way; at least what had
     happened
in other parts of the wood was sometimes more hazardous
     than pillage
in the village. But all we wanted after din-dins was a hot bath
with a squirt of Crabtree and Evelyn and a snuggle in the
     bearskin
with a pigtail. Oh you can bet I sounded off
scores of times in the Any Complaints column of the
     Chronicle;
but the brass hats, see, they were all for keeping up
     appearances:
if we didn't have him and his harp, they argued, we'd never
get another brass farthing from the Heritage Board. So on
and bloody on he had to drone. I tell you, dinosaur stew
was a piece of cake by comparison. I'm no great reader,
but give me a book any day. At least you can shut it up!

Eddie Wainwright

King of the Beasts
Wollaton Hall, Nottingham, c. 1960

In unguarded moments, I still see him jigging
his war dance, one leg rampant and one arm,
his mighty prick and balls the size of three
going on before; a vindication and a challenge.

We went down to the Hall to view him
more often than the occasion warranted,
perhaps. But it kept us entertained
and sharing, a small togetherness.

I recall your grin as you looked sideways
at his pendulum, then at me, to see
how I was taking it. Pretty well as you were,
I imagine; full of wonder, slightly envious,

somewhat revolted. I have not been back there
since your early days, nor probably have you.
But he served our turn. For all we know,
he loped off out of his glass cage,

frightening the horses, giving the women hysterics.
She would ask where we'd been. "To Wollaton,
to see the gorilla". Another sly, complicitous
smirk my way; another small secret, small bond.

I'm sure she never saw it. Just as well.

Matthew Welton

He wore a lot of corduroy and he talked a lot of crap

1. The cellist dims the pigeon-lamps.
    Demurely, in the garden-camps

    the shapes of trees the light allows
    unfold the fruits the bluefowls browse.

    The melody the morning hums
    comes only as an old thought comes.

2. The oboist who blows his cloud
    of oboe-notes and leaves them loud

    observes the way the garden-rooks
    fall from the air. The kitchen-books

    observe how well a candle's heat
    will fricassee fresh sparrow-meat.

3. Comes only as an old thought comes.
    The symphonist demurely drums

    these meanings which the morning sings.
    These meanings which the morning brings

    bring with them clouds of flies and bees
    and bluish light and bluish trees.

4. Comes only as the sounds from words,
    as flutterings of floating birds

    above the camps of clumsy cows.
    Comes only as this light allows,

    as clumsy strums by thicker thumbs
    in thickish light. But comes. But comes.

Matthew Welton

Parlour trick

The mirror in the hall reflects the spread
of junk and clutter through the room: the bed
pushed up against the wall, the paper plants,
the drop-leaf table, photos, ornaments.
A square of sunlight lengthens on the floor.

The radio, left on, purrs out some slow
six-eight, the cello with that wheezy, low
morendo that's so popular these days.
Roll up the rug, push back the chairs, this place
might make some party: dancing, drinks, the door

open onto the lawn, some darling draped
along the couch, the wall-lights dimmed. Except
if anybody did come in they'd find
the pages of the calendar unturned,
the apples clenched up in the bowl, the bulbs

all blown. The sunlight in the curtain blurs.
The lily-water yellows in the vase.
A smell like soil hangs loosely in the air.
The shelves are piled with papers; on the chair,
an uncleared plate, an ashtray filled with stubs.

Evan Gwyn Williams

A Vision of the South Wales Coal Field

1.

I came down from the mountain where the red rose
struggled darkly: walked the valley floor
through stacks of twisted metal that would impose
a pattern on my mind. This was the Spoor
of Pity I had come to track. Certain now
of that feeling, (always it came at twilight)
I searched to find the Beast, somewhere it lay low,
anger spent like money during flight.
There is a kind of passive violence
which moved me to this; participation
through thought only, like angst, as tense
as that, like this land's dark mutation.
I found the place was drilled with mine shafts deep.
The Beast lay there, I know, I heard it weep.

2.

Blaenrhondda's hills are humps, big as night
and dark as cancer. Dawn curls slowly over
them until the high sun spews its light,
the quick forged strips like brass, dense colour
of amber. Memory recalls the struck pavement,
echo of hob-nailed feet, jocular voices in
the morning air recede; enslavement
of flesh by fire, by water, blue scarred skin
of silicotic men. While concepts, laws
of Profit and Loss are played, the game
begins to pall, the huge Beast weakens, its claws
taunt only darkness, yet cast still with Cain.
Deep in one desolate and lonely mine
it lies, base and tragic symbol of its time.

Evan Gwyn Williams

Still Waters Run Deep

A dribble of river
under the forks of Canton Bridge
a farmer piking a hundred years of watery hay —
more horrid than the Styx.
If the trees were not rooted
they would run off
like the cowards they all are.

More horrid than the Somme, even,
or Passchendaele.
More horrid than the Gulag Archipelago
or the death camps
the blackened river is of fire,
of charred wood, of acrid smoke,
the furrowed black brows of a psychopathic killer.

And it hurries nowhere.

It revels in its pain —
carries less coal than my father's lungs now —
residues of a thousand Empire bound ships
that cut the seven seas like a blunt scissors.

Cleaning the mire from itself,
it cannot renew itself,
it cannot rejuvenate:
it is the sunk lung of an old otter

in endless Januaries of snow and ice:
the cut throat of the squealing pig
rending the air's metal
on the lonely farms.

It is hungrier than Moloch.

It sacrifices itself to nothing:
lives off its own foul language
in an abattoir of sunsets
that go on and on like the chaos
from which the world was born.

And it remembers nothing
except the murmer of schools of silver-bellied fish
writing an hieroglyphic of its history
no-one understands
except the river's merciless god.

With no future and no past
it enters the docks under the keels of yachts
and slips quietly away into the channel.

Only the sea knows its inner-most secrets.

John Hartley Williams

Arcadia

The glumness of the rooky wood
bends saplings into question marks.
The moon leafs back and forth. A noise is heard,
the pinging of a Chinese taxi-driver's clock.

Stopped to eat his noodles
beside the road, he's taken off his summer clothes.
Clicking chopsticks in the air, he jigs in bliss
to find how like China England is.

A dance to creaking sticklebacks
in secret ponds, to weaving frogs who score
an oriental music on their kraxing loom,
to moles who plot his gait with tumps.

Tresses of the shaggy bullroots slip
hidden visas underneath his feet.
Velvet owls hoot languidly, where
micklespit and puddock's whore embrace.

Down twilight's nude phylactery, he skips,
nettle-heedless on the ferny path
stars have painted from his taxi door
toward the mushroom kingdom of perfume.

It could be Wutungkjao or Shihkiachwang
His cabin light burns on beside a foreign road.
A dockleaf gleams inside his stinging heart.
China is his brain and England is his feet.

Who stops to scoff a noodle dish is boss.
Who belches warmly into cool, a king.
Who waltzes so priapically, a grand vizier.
Who, naked, weds a log, a sovereign lord.

John Hartley Williams

A Word from Istvan Kovács
(for Ken Smith)

Adjusting the string of my hat,
chin propped on my brass-capped stick,
I survey my pigs with a windmill eye.
When the well-pole tilts, it draws thousand year old
water from the river of my race.

Potatoes this year will be red & crisp,
fleshy to the teeth like a well-planned crime.
Peppers will be yellow & heavy,
sit in the hand like a judge's mace,
weigh down yr palm with verdicts.

I came here, you understand, with Genghis Khan
to destroy Christendom. Well, well, I thought.
You can imagine my surprise when I planted
cucumbers, beans, cauliflowers,
& they came up Christian as a girlfriend.

On a three-legged stool, by a basket of geraniums,
I wear a cloak & a woven shirt. Sunday best.
The golden clasp of my cloak is hot in the sun.
It matches the glint of my buckle.
Soon, I know, the people will come.

The donkeys put on an act of hilarity.
My cart-horse, still in the shafts, rubs its back
against a tree, tipping a wheel off the ground.
The land is flat as the vowel I use
to gee them up along the tufty track.

I see them from far off. A car across the plain.
On the high banks of the river, the trees bend & hiss.
The sky is tuned to a low resonance of wind,
like a rumour of those who resisted, the ones
who were taken away, the non-returnees.

When the guests arrive, I tip the demijohn
against my shoulder. Their eyes watch
the way it floods out — greeny-gold *kövidinka*
from the last barrel. What hospitality means
is showing the plenty you'd like to have.

I raise my glass in a cracked toast, & they try,
fumbling with the language, to repeat it.
Waiting for food, I become impatient,
let out the old familial roar of my blood
that sends the women flying into the kitchen.

'Where are you from?' I ask, imagining it,
as the women serve & retreat. The new
visitors come from the west. They praise
my viticulture. Slowly, I take my hat off
& they stare at the whiteness of my brow.

Onions might be the text for a sermon.
Garlic, the hard, white giver, its tang
richer, more forceful than a young boy's jet
might scandalise our barns this Autumn.
Shallots, I murmur, are thicker-skinned than that.

My gap-toothed grin. *Erös kolbasz*,
'Here,' I say, pushing smoked pork fat
across the table, 'you never tasted anything
like this.' I think of it sclerosing their insides
like rust on an ancient drum. I think of them

back in their own country, the futtering vitriol
slowing them, winding them down,
becoming a stone in their stomachs.
Low in the trees, from the banks of the river,
the sun chips at the quartz of my buckle.

Erös kolbasz: spicy sausage

Gregory Woods

The District Commissioner

The white man with the swagger-stick exudes authority.
  His mere moustache could halt the guilty at a thousand paces.
  A single glance from him is all we need of discipline.
When he speaks what he says has the weight of authority.
  In the shine of his boots the spittle of subordinates.
  In the lines of the uniform lion and unicorn.
His bearing underlines an absolute authority.
  Our burdensome responsibilities we pass to him.
  He carries them on shoulders reinforced with epaulettes.
The restraint in his voice holds the threat of authority.
  His influence is courted by the whole community.
  His profile is respected by the peasants in the fields.
Women in labour bend the knee to his authority.
  If he would only offer hands or trouser cuffs for kissing!
  He fathers us and we repay his care with gratitude.
The soles of his boots leave an imprint of authority.
  When we confess our lies he listens with a patient frown.
  We pray for him to intercede for us with ministers.
The parts of his body are symbols of authority.
  It pleases us to guess at how he looks without his clothes.
  We would not dare to look for fear of dying of desire.
We huddle in the shadow cast by his authority.

Gregory Woods

Nothing

The chambermaid who made the writer's bed,
When asked in court what she detected, said:

'The sheets were stained in a peculiar way.'
My lord, what more could any witness say?

The evidence was there, in brown and white,
Of what the 'nothing' they had done all night

Consisted of. Unspeakable, now spoken:
The vessel of Victorian manhood broken.

The empire fell when Wilde defiled the arse
Of an Adonis from a lower class.

Contributors' Notes

C.J. Allen's poetry has been widely published in magazines — from *Poetry Review* to *Modern Painters* — and has been broadcast on various BBC radio stations. A prize winner in numerous competitions, he has published three collections, the most recent of which is *How Copenhagen Ended* (Leafe Press, 2003) and is well-known figure on the local poetry scene.

Alan Baker was born in Newcastle-upon-Tyne and has lived in Nottingham since 1985. He publishes the Leafe Press poetry pamphlet series and runs the webzine *Litter* (www.leafepress.com/litter). He has two pamphlets in print, *The Causeway* (1999) and *Not Bondi Beach* (2002).

Adrian Buckner was born in 1962 and arrived in the Midlands via London (born) and Swansea (studied). He is the editor of *Poetry Nottingham* and a seasoned club cricketer whose best season is yet to come.

Wayne Burrows' *Marginalia,* appeared from Peterloo in 2001, and his work also featured in the British Council's *New Writing 12* (Picador, 2004). He recently completed *The Protein Songs,* a sequence about genetics for use in Retina Dance Company's *Eleven Stories About The Body,* set to tour the UK and Europe over 2005–6.

Derrick Buttress was born in Nottingham in 1932 and has always lived there. He worked as a tailor before studying English as a mature student and becoming a teacher. He is a regular in the best small magazines and his plays have been broadcast on radio and television. Shoestring published his memoir of childhood, *Broxtowe Boy,* and his recent poetry collections *Waiting for the Invasion* and *My Life as a Minor Character.*

Catherine Byron teaches writing and medieval literature at Nottingham Trent University. She grew up in Belfast and her first collection, *Settlements* (Taxus, 1985) strongly featured Irish exile. Her sixth and latest collection is *The Getting of Vellum* (Salmon Publishing, Ireland and Blackwater Press, UK, 2000).

Philip Callow is the author of fifteen novels, including *The Hosanna Man*, a story of working class life in Nottingham. His other books include biographies of Walt Whitman, Cezanne and a memoir of his Coventry childhood *Passage from Home*. His latest poetry collection is *Pastoral* (Shoestring, 2004) which came out forty years after his first.

Malcolm Carson was brought up in Lincolnshire and then in Belfast. He was editor of *Poetry Programme* while at Nottingham University in 1969-70. He now lives in Carlisle. A selection of his work appeared in the first *Take Five* from Shoestring in 2003.

Peter Cash was born in Lincolnshire on the last day of 1949. He was educated at Skegness Grammar School and Nottingham University. Since 1985, he has been Head of English Studies and Master-in-charge of 1st XI Cricket at Newcastle-under-Lyme School in Staffordshire. He received a Gregory Award in 1975 and has published five collections of poems; his most recent is *Lincolnshire Churches* (Shoestring).

Stanley Cook was a long-serving member of Nottingham Poetry Society and at different times acted as its treasurer and the editor of *Poetry Nottingham*. His collections include *Form Photograph* and *Staff Photograph*, both from Phoenix/Peterloo, and *Woods Beyond a Cornfield*, with illustrations by Rigby Graham, the Keepsake Press.

Andy Croft is the biographer of Randall Swingler, and the author of *Red Letter Days*. He is the editor of Smokestack Books and, with Adrian Mitchell, edited *Red*

Sky at Night: an anthology of socialist poetry for Five Leaves. He is editing a book of sporting poetry (with Sue Dymoke), also for Five Leaves. His own latest collection is *Comrade Laughter* (Flambard).

Joan Downar was born in London but lived in Nottinghamshire for many years. An ex-librarian and teacher, she acted and sang in the theatre and read stories for BBC Radio Nottingham. Her full collections, *The Empire of Light* (1984) and *The Old Noise of Truth* (1989) are still available from Peterloo.

Jeremy Duffield has lived in the East Midlands all his life. He has been writing since the late 1970s, mostly poetry but some plays. He has been chair of Nottingham Poetry Society for over a decade. His first full collection was *Oak Apples and Heavenly Kisses* (Headland, 2000).

Sue Dymoke lives in Nottingham and is a lecturer in education at the University of Leicester. *The New Girls*, her first full collection, was published in 2004 by Shoestring Press. Other publications include five pamphlet collections and *Drafting and Assessing Poetry* (Paul Chapman Publishing). She is editing, with Andy Croft, a book of sporting poetry for Five Leaves.

Kevin Fegan is a poet and playwright living in Mansfield. He has written over fifty plays for theatre, radio, television and film and worked as a Storyline Writer for *Coronation Street*. He has published seven volumes of poetry and is a regular performer of his own work. His collections *Racer*, *Let Your Left Hand Sing* and *Blast* are published by Five Leaves. www.kevinfegan.co.uk

Rosie Garner is a Nottingham poet best known recently for *Poetry on the Buses*; poems for the whole of the Nottingham City Transport network. Her poems have been published in magazines, appeared on many buses, and in her pamphlet collection: *We're All Here With Our Buttons Done Up Wrong*.

For many years **David Gerard** worked for the Library Services in Nottingham. Before that he had served during the second world war in the RAF as a reconnaissance photographer, a period he has written about in his memoir, *Brief Transit* (Elvet Press). In later years he lectured in Librarianship at Aberystwyth and became the bibliographer of, among others, Stanley Middleton and John Wain.

Duncan Glen is an Emeritus Professor of Nottingham Trent University. For over forty years he has been publishing poetry, mostly Scottish poetry, under the Akros imprint. For the first few years the books and magazines were set by hand with moveable type. Akros also publishes his own work. He has also written *The Poetry of the Scots* (Edinburgh University Press) and on Hugh MacDiarmid.

Cathy Grindrod is the author of *Fighting Talk* (Headland, 2005), and the pamphlet collection *Something the Heart Can't Hold* (1995). She is currently a Literature Development Officer and poetry course tutor, and has recently been appointed Poet Laureate for Derbyshire.

Madge Hales (1902-1985) lived all her life in Nottingham and was for many years associated with Nottingham Poetry Society. She was the author of two full collections, *Pine Silence* (The Fortune Press) and *Dark Landscape* (Chatto & Windus), and the pamphlet *Said the Woman: Twelve Poems* (The Byron Press). She also co-edited the literary magazine *Glass*.

John Harvey is probably best known for his two Nottingham detective series based round the detectives Resnick and Frank Elder. He was the editor of *Slow Dancer* and his own jazz influenced poetry appears in *Bluer Than This* and *Ghosts of a Chance*. www.mellotone.co.uk

Keith Howden was born in Burnley, 1932. He lectured 1966-1989 at, ultimately, Nottingham Trent University, with a major interest in formalist approaches to modern European literature. He has published two collections: *Marches of Familiar Landscape* and *Onkonkay* both with Peterloo. Now retired and, while still writing, is more preoccupied with painting.

Pamela Lewis has been widely published and broadcast since her first collection *One Mile from the Centre*. She wrote a series of poems to mark the D.H. Lawrence celebrations, Cycle for a Centenary. She spends much of her time travelling and reflecting on the poetry of place.

John Lucas is the author of many books of a critical and scholarly nature, including *The Radical Twenties* published by Five Leaves, and of seven collections of poetry, including *Studying Grosz On the Bus*, winner of the Aldeburgh Poetry Prize in 1990 and, more recently, *The Long and the Short Of It* (2004). In 1994 he founded Shoestring Press.

Julie Lumsden has lived in Nottingham for many years. Between 2001-2004 she edited *Poetry Nottingham*. Her own work has appeared in numerous magazines and a pamphlet collection, *Naked by Profession*, is available from Leafe Press. In 2004, BBC Radio Four broadcast her first radio play.

Clare MacDonald Shaw is the author of two collections of poems, *How Ghosts Begin* (Shoestring, 1997) and *Blue Fever* (Blackwater, 1999). She read English at Oxford, has taught in London, America and Nottingham and was editor of the magazine *Quartz*.

Jamie McKendrick, a student at Nottingham University from 1972-5, won the 1997 Forward Prize for Best Collection with *The Marble Fly*. A selection of his poems is available in *Sky Nails: Poems 1979-1997* and his latest collection is *Ink Stone*, both Faber. He is also the editor of *Twentieth Century Italian Poems*.

Stanley Middleton was born in 1919 in Bulwell, Nottingham. Married with two daughters, he attended the University of Nottingham from 1938-40 and from 1946-7, subsequently teaching until 1981. Stanley Middleton has published more than forty novels, most recently *Sterner Stuff*. His *Holiday* (now available from Five Leaves) won the Booker Prize in 1974. The poems in this collection were written in his 20s

Blake Morrison was born in Yorkshire and educated at Nottingham University. He has published critical works, play scripts, memoir, libretti and a novel. His most recent poetry publication, *Pendle Witches* was illustrated by Paula Rego. He is a former chair of the Poetry Book Society and editor (with Andrew Motion) of *The Penguin Book of Contemporary British Poetry*.

Peter Mortimer has been running Iron Press (www.ironpress.co.uk) since 1973. Born in Nottingham, he lives in the North East where he is also a playwright and travel writer. His books include *Broke Through Britain*. His most recent poetry collection, *I Married the Angel of the North*, was published by Five Leaves who will also publish his *Off the Wall* — a play and travelogue about Hadrian's Wall.

Graham Mort, who was both a student and gardener at Nottingham University, is director for postgraduate studies in creative writing at Lancaster University. He is a specialist in distance learning and leads the African writers mentoring scheme 'Crossing Borders'. Two of his poetry collections have involved collaboration with visual artists and his latest collection is *A Night on the Lash* (Seren, 2004).

Michael Murphy was a research student at Nottingham Trent University, and the author of two poetry collections from Shoestring. He edited *The Collected George Garrett* for Trent Editions. His latest book is *Poetry in Exile: a study of the poetry of W.H. Auden, Joseph Brodsky and*

146

George Szirtes (Greenwich Exchange, 2004). Recent poems appear in *New Irish Poets* (Bloodaxe).

Henry Normal comes from Nottingham and now lives in Brighton. He founded the Manchester Poetry Festival in 1994 and was a regular on the poetry performance circuit, publishing a series of collections. These days he mainly works with Steve Coogan as a script writer in their script-writing and production company Baby Cow. His latest poetry-related work was the series *Whine Gums* for BBC 3.

Betty Parvin, for many years a stalwart of Nottingham Poetry Society, published a number of short collections, including *The Bird with the Luck* (The Byron Press, 1968). Her poems appeared in a wide variety of magazines in both the UK and the USA.

Tom Paulin lectured in English at Nottingham University from 1972-89 and was Reader in Poetry until 1994. His earlier poems often reflected on the political situation in Northern Ireland. He is a regular contributor to radio and television. His latest poetry collection, *The Road to Inver*, which was short-listed for the 2004 Forward Prize, brings together work from four decades.

Nigel Pickard was born in West Germany in 1966 but has lived and worked in Nottingham for fifteen years. His first poetry collection, *Making Sense*, was published by Shoestring in 2004, his first novel, *One*, by Bookcase Editions in 2005.

Peter Porter was born in Brisbane — of Nottingham descent — and moved to London in 1951. During the 1950s he was associated with "The Group", his first collection appearing in 1961. Many collections and awards have followed, his most recent being *Afterburner* (Picador, 2004). For the last seven years he has been a Visiting Professor at Nottingham Trent University.

Allan Rodway was Reader in English at Nottingham University. Primarily known as a critic, his books include *The Romantic Conflict*, *A Preface to Auden*, *Truths of Fiction* and *English Comedy: from Chaucer to the Present*, as well as *Poetry of the 1930s*. His poems are represented in *Two Poets* (The Byron Press, 1965) and, from the same publisher, *Continuities*, 1978.

Peter Sansom, brought up in north Nottinghamshire, is a Creative Writing Fellow at the University of Leeds and is the editor of *The North* and Smith/Doorstep Books. He is the author of three collections of poetry and of *Writing Poems* (Bloodaxe), and is a Director of The Poetry Business.

Vernon Scannell, whose childhood years were spent in Beeston, was the recipient of the Heinemann Award for Literature in 1960. His many collections include *The Loving Game* which was Poetry Book Society Choice. His latest collection is *Behind the Lines* (Shoestring Press, 2004).

Alan Sillitoe has written eight volumes of poetry, with a ninth due for publication. His best known fiction includes the classic Nottingham novel *Saturday Night and Sunday Morning* and *The Loneliness of the Long Distance Runner* which were published in 1958 and 1959. He is still publishing novels, essays and reviews.

Sheila Smith taught at Nottingham University and has written poems since adolescence. She founded the organisation Art to Share, a society committed to providing access to the arts for the blind, partially-sighted and sighted coming together to enjoy and practise them. Her collection *Chalk and Cheese* was published by Shoestring in 2001.

Mahendra Solanki was born in 1956 in Nairobi of Indian parents. He teaches on the MA in Creative Writing at Nottingham Trent University. His two collections of poetry are *Shadows of My Making* (Lokamaya Press, 1986) and *What You Leave Behind* (Blackwater Press, 1996).

Michael Standen attended High Pavement School in Nottingham before being conscripted into the army. Most of his working life has been within adult education, especially the WEA. He lives in Durham where he is managing editor of *Other Poetry*. As well as poetry, he has written several novels for adults and younger readers. His latest collection is *Gifts of Egypt* (Shoestring Press).

Martin Stannard's most recent collections of poetry are *Coral* (Leafe Press, 2004) and *Difficulties and Exultations* (Smith/Doorstep, 2001). Recently he has been running a website of poetry, reviews and comment, *Exultations and Difficulties* at www.exultationsanddifficulties.blogspot.com. He is currently teaching English in China.

Jenny Swann studied English literature and art history, and works as a freelance writer and art historian. Her Flambard collection *Soft Landings* was a *City Life* book of the year. She now lives in Nottingham, where Shoestring Press has published her latest collection *Stay*.

Deborah Tyler-Bennett's local roots helped generate her first collection *Clark Gable in Mansfield*. She is a part-time English lecturer at Loughborough University and editor of the literary magazine *The Coffee House*. Her book *Edith Sitwell: the forgotten modernist* was published by Sheffield Hallam University Press.

Hugh Underhill is a graduate of Nottingham University with two collections of poetry from Nottinghamshire presses: *The World We Make* (Shoestring Press, 1996), *The Actual Hour* (Poetry Monthly Press, 2001). His other publications include *The Problem of Consciousness in Modern Poetry* (CUP, 1992) and *Passing Through Glass* (National Poetry Foundation, 1997). He edits *The Robert Bloomfield Society Newsletter*.

Eddie Wainwright was Head of English at Forest Fields Grammar School, Nottingham, from 1957 to 1961, and was Principal Lecturer at Nottingham College of Education from 1961-69. He has published poems and articles in many magazines and anthologies and is about to publish, with Lapwing Press, his sixth poetry collection.

Matthew Welton's *The Book of Matthew* won the Jerwood-Aldeburgh first collection prize. Born in Nottinghamshire, he now lives in Manchester and teaches creative writing at the University of Bolton. He was co-editor of *Stand* from 2002-2004.

Evan Gwyn Williams was born in 1938 in Neath but has lived in Nottinghamshire for many years. He was a member of the Group Poetry Workshop which included Peter Porter, George MacBeth, Alan Brownjohn and Philip Hobsbaum. He is an elected member of the Academi Cymraeg and his latest collection is *Mammon* (Tuba Press, 2003).

John Hartley Williams has published eight collections of poetry, most recently *Blues* (Cape, 2004), short-listed for the Forward Prize. A graduate from Nottingham University, he teaches English at the Free University of Berlin, where he has lived since 1976 and where he has also organised many poetry readings and festivals.

Gregory Woods has published three poetry collections: *We Have the Melon*, *May I Say Nothing* and *The District Commissioner's Dreams,* all with Carcanet Press. His critical books include *A History of Gay Literature*, from Yale University Press. He is Professor of Gay and Lesbian Studies at Nottingham Trent University.

Acknowledgements

Alan Baker's poems are taken from *Not Bondi Beach* (Leafe Press); Adrian Buckner's poems appear in *One Man Queue* (Leafe Press); Wayne Burrows' 'Side-Effects' appeared in *Tabla Book of New Verse 2001* and 'A Recipe for Insanity' is taken from *Marginalia* (Peterloo Poets, 2001); Derrick Buttress' 'Sealed with a Loving Kiss, 1944' appears in *My Life as a Minor Character* (Shoestring); Philip Callow's 'Pastoral' is the title poem of his Shoestring collection; Catherine Byron's 'The Blue Darkness' is from *The Getting of Vellum* (Blackwater) and 'This was *Halal*' from the *Fat-Hen Field Hospital* (Lockwood Stoneleigh); Malcolm Carson's poems are included in *Take Five 03* (Shoestring); Peter Cash's poems appear in *Lincolnshire Churches* (Shoestring); Stanley Cook's poems are both from *Form Photograph* (Phoenix Pamphlet Poets); Andy Croft's 'My Favourite Martian' is from *Nowhere Special* (Flambard) and 'Methuselah's Losers' from *Just as Blue* (Flambard); Joan Downar's poems were published in *Critical Survey*; Jeremy Duffield's poems were taken from *Oak Apples and Heavenly Kisses* (Headland); Sue Dymoke's 'The Undertaking' appears in *The New Girls* (Shoestring); Kevin Fegan's poems comprise part of *Matey Boy* (Iron Press); Rosie Garner's poems are from *We're All Here, with Our Buttons Done Up Wrong*; David Gerard's poems are from *Pillow Talk* (Elvet Press, 2005); Duncan Glen's poems are from *A Selection of Poems* and *Selected New Poems 1987-1996* (both Akros); Cathy Grindrod's 'Taking Tea with Byron' is from *Fighting Talk* (Headland) and 'Exposure' is from the Lancaster Poetry Competition prizewinners anthology and Second Light; Madge Hales' poems appeared in *Ambit 99*; John Harvey's poems are from *Bluer Than This* (Smith/Doorstop); John Lucas' 'An Irregular Ode...' is from *One for the Piano* (Redbeck) and 'Reading Ovid in Beeston' is from *The Long and the Short Of It* (Redbeck); Julie Lumsden's 'Skegness and Global Warming' is from *Sixteen Poems* (Open House Editions); Clare MacDonald Shaw's poems are from *Blue Fever* (Blackwater); Jamie McKendrick's 'Home Thoughts' is from *The Kiosk on the Brink* and 'Banana Boat' is from *The Marble Fly* (both OUP); Blake Morrison's 'Grange Boy' appeared in *Dark Glasses* and 'The Kiss' in *The Ballad of the Yorkshire Ripper* (both Chatto); Graham Mort's 'Storm Larks' appears in *Circular Breathing* (Dangaroo), 'Geese from a Timber House' in *A Night on the Lash* (Seren); Michael Murphy's poems are from *Elsewhere*

(Shoestring); Henry Normal's 'Experiments with Worms' appears in *The Fifteenth of February* (AK Press) while 'The Last Poem I Ever Wrote' first appeared in *Love Like Hell* (A Twist in the Tale); Betty Parvin's poems appeared in *The Bird with the Luck* (Byron Press); Tom Paulin's poems are both from *A State of Justice* (Faber); Nigel Pickard's poems appear in *Making Sense* (Shoestring); Peter Porter's 'Addio Senza Rancor' is from *English Subtitles* (OUP) and 'Good Vibes' is taken from *Living in a Calm Country* (OUP); Allan Rodway's poems were included in *Continuities* (Byron Press); Vernon Scannell's 'Autobiographical Note' was included in his *Selected Poems* (Allison & Busby) and 'A Numinous Event' in *Behind the Lines* (Shoestring); Alan Sillitoe's 'Oxney' and 'Lancaster' appear in his *Collected Poems* (HarperCollins); Mahendra Solanki's poems are from *What You Leave Behind* (Blackwater); Michael Standen's 'Last' is from *Time's Fly-Past* (Flambard) and 'What Eng. Lit. Did for Me' is from *Gifts of Egypt* (Shoestring); Jenny Swann's 'The Discuss Thrower' is taken from *Soft Landings* (Flambard) and 'Bread and Butter Pudding' from *Stay* (Shoestring); Deborah Tyler-Bennett's poems appear in *Clark Gable in Mansfield: Selected Poems* (King's England Press); Eddie Wainwright's 'Bearding the Bard' first appeared in *Poetry Monthly*; Matthew Welton's poems were published in *The Book of Matthew* by Matthew Welton (Carcanet Press Limited, 2003); Evan Gwyn Williams' 'A Vision of the South Wales Coal Field' is from *The Invocation of Manawydan* (Shoestring) and 'Still Waters Run Deep' from *Mammon* (Tuba Press); John Hartley Williams' 'Arcadia' is from *Blues* (Cape) while 'A Word for Istvan Kovács' appears in *Canada* (Bloodaxe); 'The District Commissioner' and 'Nothing' by Gregory Woods appear respectively in *The District Commissioner's Dreams* and *May I Say Nothing* (Carcanet Press Limited, 2002 and 1998).

Other poems are published here for the first time.